Tai Shing Pek Kwar

MONKEY KUNG-FU

by Paulie Zink and Michael J. Gonzalez

DISCLAIMER

Please note that the publisher of this instructional book is NOT RESPONSIBLE in any manner whatsoever for any injury which may occur by reading and/or following the instructions herein.

It is essential that before following any of the activities, physical or otherwise, herein described, the reader or readers should first consult his or her physician for advice on whether or not the reader or readers should embark on the physical activity described herein. Since the physical activities described herein may be too sophisticated in nature, it is essential that a physician be consulted.

UNIQUE PUBLICATIONS
4201 Vanowen Place
Burbank, CA 91505

ISBN: 0-86568-061-2
Library of Congress Catalog Number: 84-52682

Published 1986. Printed in the United States of America.
Designer: Danilo J. Silverio
Editors: Sandra Segal and Dave Cater

DEDICATION

To my master, Jim Cho Chat Ling. I am eternally grateful to him for teaching me the true way — not only in martial arts, but also in life.

PREFACE

And here it is. To my knowledge, this is the most complete book ever written about the history and practice of this rare art. Because I've received an overwhelming number of requests for more information about the history, training methods, techniques, and everything involved in tai shing pek kwar, I was encouraged to write it all down on paper.

According to martial arts tradition, especially as reported in the magazines, only an Asian can be the master of an art. I don't feel that's necessarily true or fair. I feel that anyone can master a style if his attitude is right and his spirit is willing.

While I was dabbling in the martial arts at an early age, a great master took the time to teach me this art, which had been handed down to him from his family. I don't teach commercially because I feel that techniques may become watered down in the process. I believe that by having only a small group of disciples, I can keep the art as close to tradition as possible.

However, because I am the only known tai shing pek kwar master in America, I feel a responsibility to share my art. Since it's very hard to answer questions or demonstrate techniques for someone outside of my state — California — I will use these pages to reach out and pass on information to all those who are interested in tai shing pek kwar.

TABLE OF CONTENTS

TAI SHING PEK KWAR FAMILY TREE

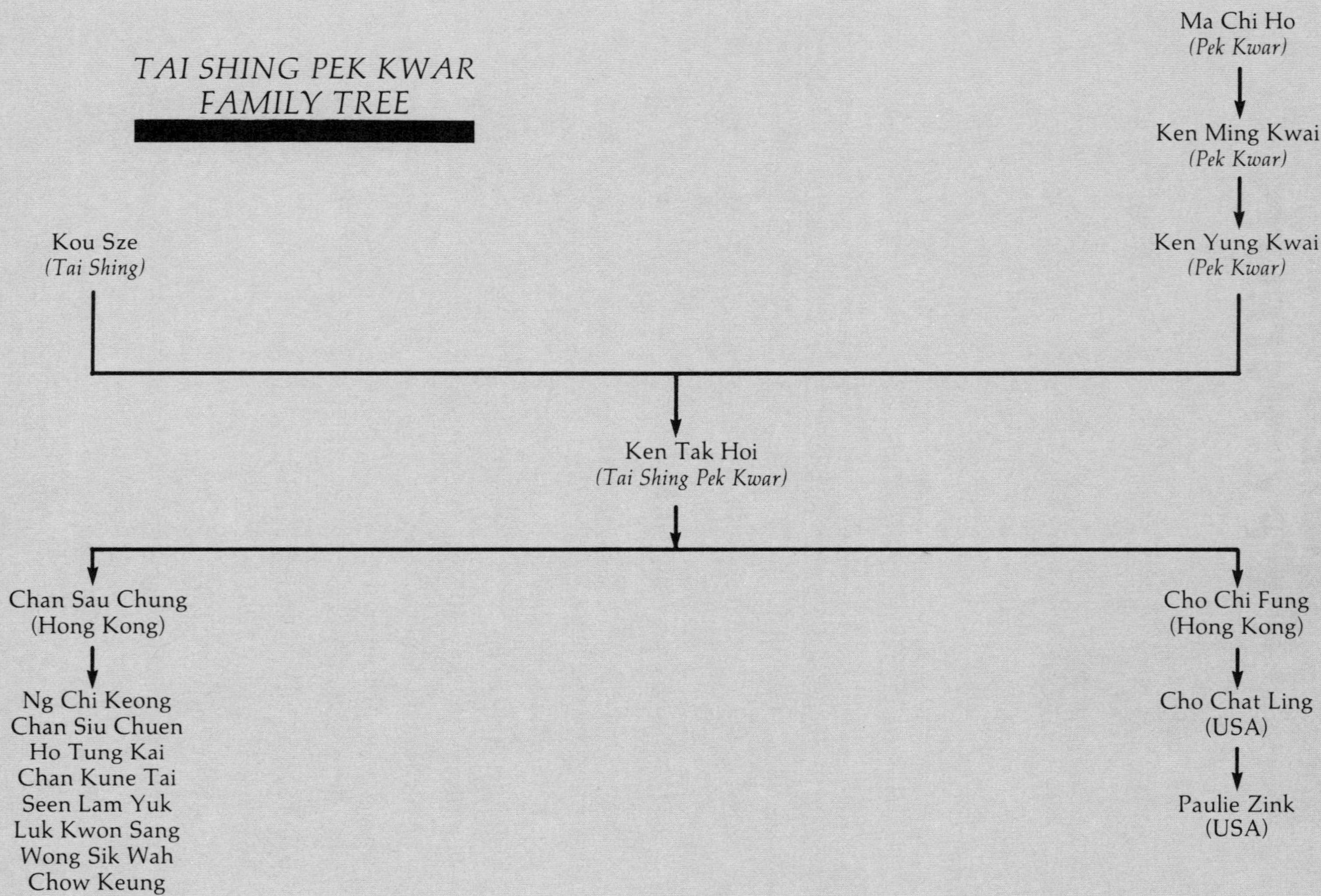

INTRODUCTION

Tai shing pek kwar, or monkey style kung-fu as it is better known, is considered one of the most unusual and effective styles of kung-fu. Its deceiving and unorthodox techniques make it an awesome and strange sight to behold.

Though many kung-fu styles are based on the characteristics of animals, such as the Shaolin five animals, tai shing pek kwar, which is based on the antics of the monkeys, is set apart from all other animal styles. To master this art, the practitioner must become a monkey — mentally — rather than just imitating one.

Monkey kung-fu is made up of two separate and complete arts, tai shing (monkey style), and pek kwar (ax-fist style). It is perhaps one of the most difficult arts to learn, requiring the utmost in skill, flexibility, and physical and mental control. The style is divided into five forms or five monkey characteristics. These include the "tall monkey," "lost monkey," "stone monkey," "drunken monkey," and "wooden monkey."

Each form is characterized by low stances and sudden attacks. In studying tai shing pek kwar, the practitioner first learns the art of pek kwar and several of the monkey exercises. Later, the instructor will choose one of the five monkey forms for the student to master. It takes several years to master even one.

This book will explain the movements and function of each monkey form, the prerequisites for studying each form, and the colorful weaponry of tai shing pek kwar, which has been kept secret for decades.

THE HISTORY OF TAI SHING PEK KWAR

As mentioned earlier, the art of tai shing pek kwar is made up of two separate and complete arts: tai shing (monkey style), which was founded by Master Kou Sze, and pek kwar (ax-fist style), which was founded by Master Ma Chi Ho.

Pek Kwar Style

The art of pek kwar was founded over 200 years ago by Master Ma Chi Ho, who lived in Shantung province. He based this particular style of pek kwar kung-fu on ax-fist techniques which use circular long arm and free-swinging movements, low stances, and the internal energy of chi. It is not a pretty or flashy style, but it's filled with the quick and powerful movements of sudden blows and strikes. The style uses circular patterns and angular strikes, resembling those made by a man swinging an ax in each hand.

While Ma Chi Ho was quite young, he lived down the road from a nearby Taoist temple. Out of the kindness of his heart, young Ma would gather and chop wood for the priests who lived in that temple.

One day, one of the priests from the temple approached Ma and said to him, "Metal may conquer wood, but the spirit is stronger." Then the priest walked away without giving an explanation of this saying. Though Ma was puzzled, he still continued his chore of chopping wood to provide for the priests.

With an ax in each hand — which helped double the results — he chopped at the limbs of every tree he could reach. Later, when Ma decided he had gathered enough wood for the temple that day, he slowly set both his axes down. Then the priest's saying suddenly came to mind. "Metal may conquer wood, but the spirit is stronger."

Ma sat down on a log and studied the saying. "Metal," thought Ma to himself, "must mean the ax in my hand and the conquering of wood must be my chopping off branches. The the spirit must mean me, or the inner me, which is stronger."

Ma then took one of the axes in his hand and swung it at one of the branches of the tree, chopping it off. He set down the ax and walked up to the tree. After angling his arm and his fists, as if he were using an ax, he swung at the branch. To his amazement, the limb broke off.

Through this realization that he could wield his strength and inner spirit like an ax, Ma later perfected a new type of free-swinging motion. Ma combined these motions with several of the Northern kung-fu styles that he knew into a brand-new style. He named it pek kwar or ax-fist style.

Ma Chi Ho later passed on this art to his protege Ken Ming Kwai, who passed it to his son, Ken Yung Kwai, who then passed it on to his son, Ken Tak Hoi.

Tai Shing Style

The history of tai shing kung-fu begins at the turn of the century, near the end of the Ching dynasty (1644-1911). At this time, a famous short-tempered kung-fu fighter from Northern China, by the name of Kou Sze, was imprisoned for killing an evil fellow villager in a fight. Punishment for someone found guilty of such a crime was either death or life imprisonment. To save Kou Sze from either penalty, several of his closest and influential friends got together and managed to bribe the judge to reduce Kou Sze's sentence to only eight years in prison. Kou Sze was placed in solitary confinement to serve out his eight-year prison term. To pass the time away, Kou Sze trained intensively in some of the Northern kung-fu styles he had learned, particularly in tei tong (great earth style), named for its ground fighting techniques.

The prison in which Kou Sze was held was located in a forest on the outskirts of town. By a strange fate, the cell window faced a grove of tall trees inhabited by a colony of chattering monkeys frolicking and swinging from tree to tree. Fascinated by the monkeys' playful antics among the branches, Kou Sze spent hours observing the little animals. Soon he began to analyze every action of the monkeys.

He discovered that not all monkeys were alike. Each had a different personality and different characteristics. Each responded differently to different situations. Playful monkeys, for instance, behaved quite differently when playfully fighting with one another than when actually fighting other animals.

Kou Sze realized that these monkeys' antics were compatible with the tei tong style he had learned from childhood. After intensively studying every movement and action of each of the monkeys and incorporating these movements with the tei tong style, Kou Sze founded a new and unusual fighting method he called tai shing (great sage), so named in honor of Sun Wu Kung, the monkey king in the Chinese folktale "Journey to the West."

Through careful study, Kou Sze was able to break down all of the monkeys' reactions and categorize them into five different personality types. Thereby he founded five different forms: the tall monkey, the lost monkey, the drunken monkey, the wooden monkey and the stone monkey forms. These five forms make up the tai shing art.

Unlike other systems of kung-fu, tai shing has its own principles of maneuvering, including grabbing, falling, lunging, and light art jumping and turning. In addition, there are six principles of mental attitude that must be cultivated in this art. They include deviousness, elusiveness, unpredictability, sneakiness, and destructiveness. Each of these is employed in each of the five monkey forms. However, each monkey has a unique method of fighting.

The tall monkey form, for instance, resembles the fighting style of the tallest monkey in a clan. Taking advantage of his long legs and arms, he would reach out to strike an opponent.

By being just able to keep out of his foe's reach, he would not allow himself to get hit.

The tall monkey form consists of circular swinging patterns similar to long-range kung-fu styles. However, the tall monkey can also appear to be quite small, tucking himself in like a little ball, then suddenly springing out for an attack. The tall monkey form is best suited for a tall student of the art.

Another monkey that fascinated Kou was a little frightened monkey that got separated from the other group of monkeys. After being lost for a long period of time, the little monkey became extremely frightened, startled by any noise and always looking around. Yet, even in this frightened state, instead of panicking when confronted by larger beasts, the monkey managed to successfully defend himself and flee from danger. Kou Sze called the techniques based on these observations the lost monkey form.

The lost monkey appears to be innocent and confused. But he is actually tricky and deceiving. The form includes footwork and movements which are extremely quick and flexible.

The drunken monkey is the most unorthodox fighting method. This form is based on the behavior of an intoxicated monkey. Known for their curiosity, the monkeys would often sneak into a nearby village to pick up any scraps of food they could find. They would eat and drink anything they could get their hands on — including wine, when available.

When drunk, the monkey is usually sick and dizzy. His posture is unbalanced, and he frequently stumbles and falls, making him easy prey for a hungry beast.

With these erratic swaying and falling steps in mind, Kou Sze founded the broken rhythm type of combat. The practitioner must learn how to fight effectively while in this sort of "drunk" state. Swaying, staggering, lunging and falling, the stylist looks like easy prey. But while he may seem to have lost control and balance, he must always be ready for attack. The stylist must have a spiritual drunkeness rather than a physical drunkeness. He must still have all his speed and power, but must hide it in broken steps and motions and not use it until necessary. These strange and unusual tactics baffle and confuse most other fighters because of the unpredictable movements and attacks.

The wood monkey is best described in one word: sneaky. This form is considered the most deceptive and aggressive. Its movements and attacks are hidden in a cloak of deception.

While serving out his prison term, Kou Sze often noticed a monkey being chased by a much larger beast. In some cases, the monkey that was being chased would suddenly stop, turn around and attack the beast. Surprised, the beast would be completely open. Usually, he was the one to flee the monkey's attack. Leading the opponent on, then turning around and capitalizing on his surprise, is the main characteristic of this form.

The final monkey form is the stone monkey, which relies on endurance and brute strength.

Kou Sze noticed that in every colony of monkeys there was always a "tough guy," usually the leader. He would always be the first at everything, the most daring, the most courageous. He was strong, not timid like so many of the others.

This form is the most brutal in monkey kung-fu. It uses techniques that are hard on the body, such as body flops and somersaults, which can be damaging to the knee, elbow and ankle joints. For this reason, only the strongest students can successfully learn this form.

The stone monkey uses force against force, and so the student must condition his body to be resilient to blows, when exchanging punches one-on-one. The stone monkey has the attitude or spirit of being tough and hard as a rock.

A monkey stylist who is able to master all five forms would truly be a versatile fighter. But since each of the monkeys has its own personality, a master of tai shing would select only one of the five monkey forms for a student to master; one that best fits the student's physique and personality. Thus, mastering one form is completely mastering the tai shing art for that student.

After serving his term, Kou Sze handed down his new style of fighting to his best friend's son, Ken Tak Hoi, a master of pek kwar (ax-fist). Later, when Ken Tak Hoi opened a school in China, he combined the monkey style with his style and called it tai shing pek kwar.

Throughout Ken Tak Hoi's years of teaching, he jealously concealed tai shing boxing, but openly taught pek kwar. Only those who completely mastered pek kwar, and happened to be a close friend or relative, would learn the tai shing art.

When Ken Tak Hoi died, no successor had been named to carry on the school. Those close friends and relatives to whom

Ken Tak Hoi had entrusted the knowledge of all five forms of the monkey style usually kept it secret and passed it on only to their heirs.

One of Ken Tak Hoi's close friends, and also a senior student of the tai shing pek kwar school, Cho Chi Fung, passed on this rare art to his nephew, Cho Chat Ling. When he came to America, Cho passed it on to his only student, Paulie Zink.

Today, Zink guards the tradition of tai shing pek kwar. He teaches pek kwar, then tai shing only to a select few to keep the art as close to tradition as possible.

THE ROLE OF FLEXIBILITY

Stretching is one of the best things you can do for your body to get it ready for strenuous exercise. But in the martial arts world, a stretch period is often considered the most boring class routine, and taking ten precious minutes or longer to limber up your body is referred to as a waste of time. In most schools, stretching consists of a few minutes of warm-ups. A couple of head and arm twirls, lean to the right, lean to the left, and now you're ready. Little importance is placed on what stretching can do for your body. In many cases, the instructor uses improper stretching techniques, which may do more harm than good.

Those of us who do attempt to travel down this "limber" road of flexibility realize that there's something more to stretching than just being able to extend your body further than before. Stretching gives you extra power, as it allows a flow of energy through the entire body. Stretching also develops internal power, often called *chi kung*, when it is combined with certain breathing methods. Flexibility enhances physical strength, enabling you to execute techniques with flowing movements rather than hard and rigid motions, and still have same, or an even greater amount of power. Endurance, mobility, balance, and inner strength also come from greater flexibility.

In tai shing pek kwar, flexibility is of major importance. In an average four-hour class period, stretching exercises are not just a "quick flex" time — they make take up to two hours.

A high degree of flexibility is required for each of the five monkey forms. Flexibility of the ankles plays an important role in low stances and mobility. Circular sweeping and kicking requires an extreme amount of leg flexibility. In fact, nearly every part of the body must be stretched in one way or another, because each move in tai shing pek kwar requires flexibility to perform it properly. The stretching techniques used in this art include the front and sidesplits, the chin-to-toe stretch, and the stretch in which the foot is placed over the head, a highly difficult technique. Back flexibility is vital for the flow of energy.

Breathing is another important factor in learning how to stretch. By breathing correctly through your nose, you can control your heartbeat, and in this way build endurance. Breathing should always be slow, rhythmical and cyclical — let tha air flow from your nose, through your body to your *dan tien* (abdominal area), up your back and then back out through your nose.

If you are bending forward to do a stretch, exhale as you bend forward. Then breathe slowly as you hold the stretch. Do not hold your breath while stretching. Relaxing while stretching will tremendously improve your flexibility while helping you to breathe properly. Once you learn to relax, your body will slowly move into wider and longer positions. If a stretch position inhibits your breathing pattern, then ease up on the stretch so you can breathe freely.

Bouncing up and down is a big no-no. It puts a strain on your muscles and creates a stretch reflex — tightening the very muscles you are trying to stretch. These harmful methods cause pain, as well as damage to the muscle tissues.

You can also damage yourself if you rush into a stretch and push your body beyond what it is used to. You must let your body adapt slowly to the stretch or you can seriously damage the delicate muscle tissues.

In one case, a young student wanted so much to impress the instructor with her progress in stretching that she jumped into the air and forced herself into a sidesplits — which she had never previously been able to do. She tore the muscles and tendons in her legs so severely that she was crippled for a long time.

Proper instruction in stretching is a must for effective development of the body. Learning the dos and don'ts of stretching can save your body from unwanted pain, injury, and muscle scars.

When beginning a stretch, spend about 30 seconds in a simple or easy stretch. This will get your body used to the idea that it's going to be stretched, ready the tissues for stretching and loosen the muscles. Then hold your stretch for 60 seconds as you slowly move to the point where you feel a mild bit of tension. As you hold that stretch, relax to let your body adapt to the new position. Never rush into a stretch or jump down and force yourself into a stretch. Never jerk, bob, or bounce. Work your way into a stretch.

At first, count out the seconds for each stretch. This will ensure that you hold the proper tension long enough. After awhile, you will know how long to hold the stretch by the way it feels to you, without the distraction of counting. If you stretch correctly and regularly, you will find that every movement you make becomes much easier.

As you continue to stretch, you may notice what is often called a breakthrough. This occurs after you have stretched yourself to a certain point and are unable to stretch past it. As time goes by, you begin to notice that you find it hard reaching that point again. After awhile, when you attempt to reach that point again, your body not only reaches that point but this time goes quite a bit further. This happens because your tendons first begin to loosen up, and then suddenly tighten up again — but only to prepare to loosen up further. Your stretch will go further when the tendons re-release.

Stretching exercises require patience, time, endurance and above all, consistency. You will find that if you stretch regularly, your flexibility will naturally increase. Daily stretching speeds your progress even more.

Anyone can really learn how to stretch, regardless of his age or present flexibility. It's a myth that you can only stretch when you're young. The person's age, weight, height, sex, or physique makes no difference in learning how to stretch. No one is too heavy or too muscular to stretch; anybody who is willing can do it.

Advanced flexibility techniques should only be attempted after several of the basic stretches have been mastered. The advanced techniques combine the internal breathing cycles, a deep state of meditation, and one of the more advanced stretches, such as the splits or the advanced leg stretch, held for a long period.

A student begins by holding one position for about five-to-ten minutes. After achieving a degree of comfort and flexibility, the student increases the time holding each posture to one hour.

Some of the unusual names for these postures include the "Great Sage Seeking the Silver Frost," and the "Green Silken Cord Meditation."

Basic Stretching

1

Stretching is one of the most vital parts of the monkey style of kung-fu. The first position of the basic stretch is standing upright with feet approximately three feet apart.

2

With your hands making fists, gently and slowly lean your upper body forward with both arms pointed toward the ground.

3

The fists should be touching the ground at this point. Do not arch your back; keep your back straight and your head up.

4

Slowly bring in feet step by step until they are touching. Your upper body should move closer to your legs.

5

Place your hands behind each ankle and pull your upper body so that it touches your legs. This position should be held for at least 30 seconds and repeated several times.

Chin-to-toe stretch

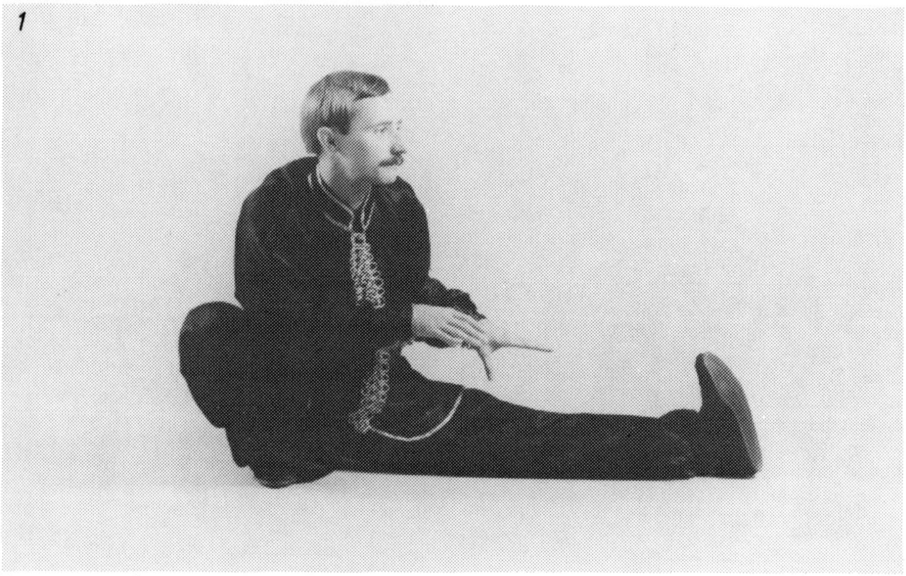

Beginning from a ground position, your right leg should be bent with right foot flat and your left leg flat on the ground. Your toes are pointed up.

Lean your upper body toward your left leg. Reaching out with your right hand, grab your leg just below the left knee.

Continue to lean your body forward, keeping your right hand on your left leg. Reach out with your left hand and grab the instep of your foot.

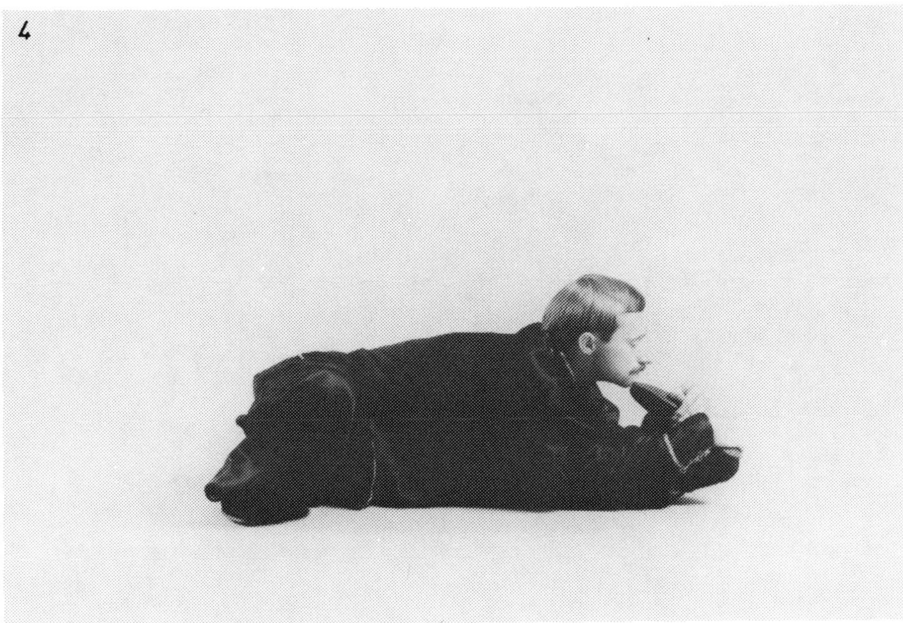

With your right hand, grab the instep of your foot. Both hands should be holding the insteps. Bring your head down until you touch your chin to your toes, all the while stretching your left ankle toward you.

5

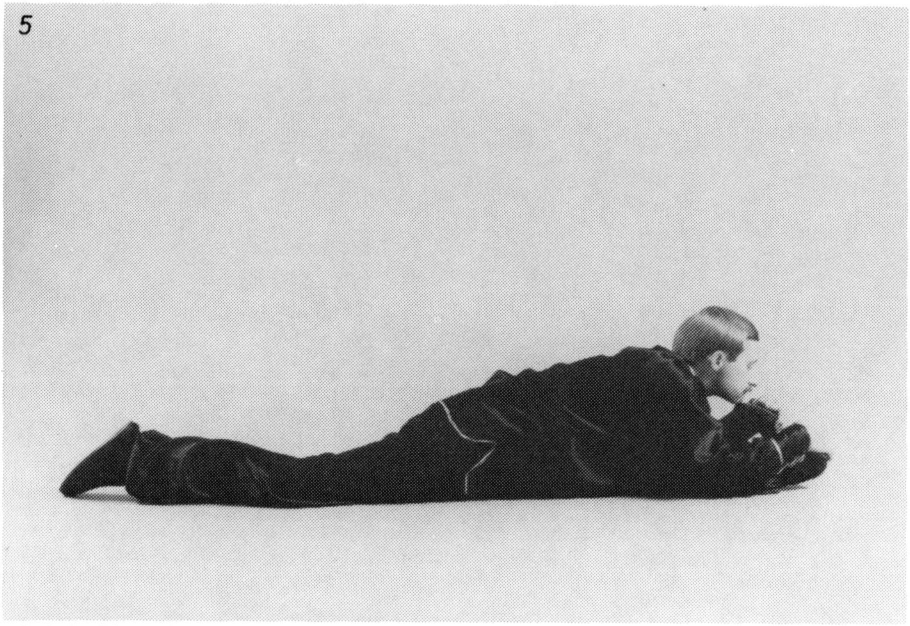

While holding this position, bring your right leg back very slowly to a splits position, keeping your chin to your toe.

6

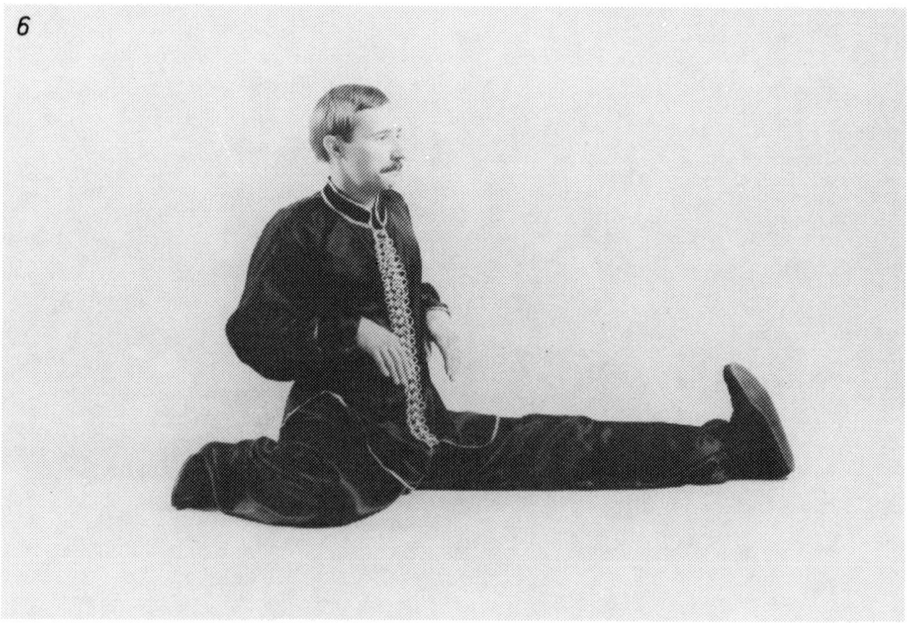

To make this stretch easier, place your right knee to the ground and make your right foot flat.

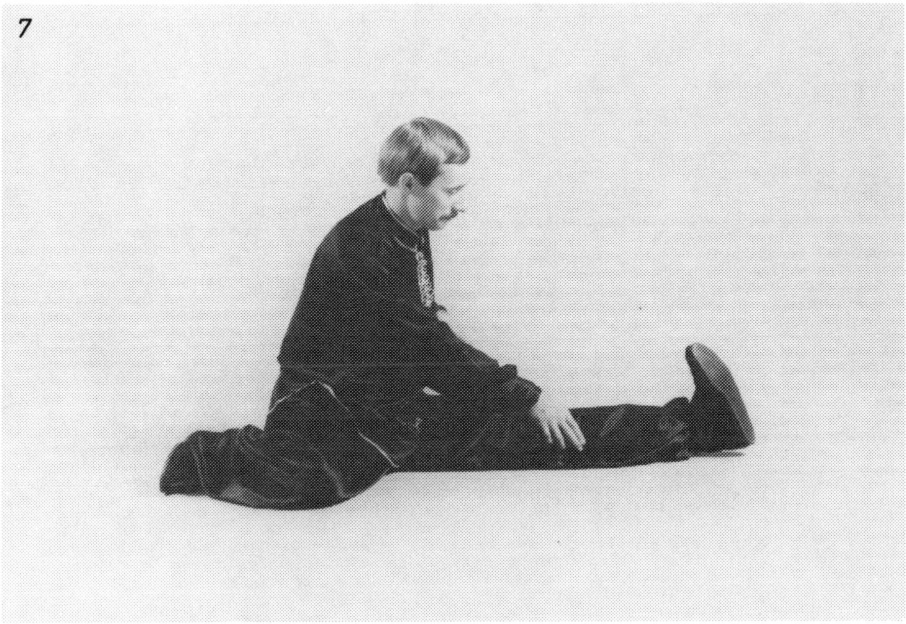

Grab your knee with your right hand and bend your left ankle toward you.

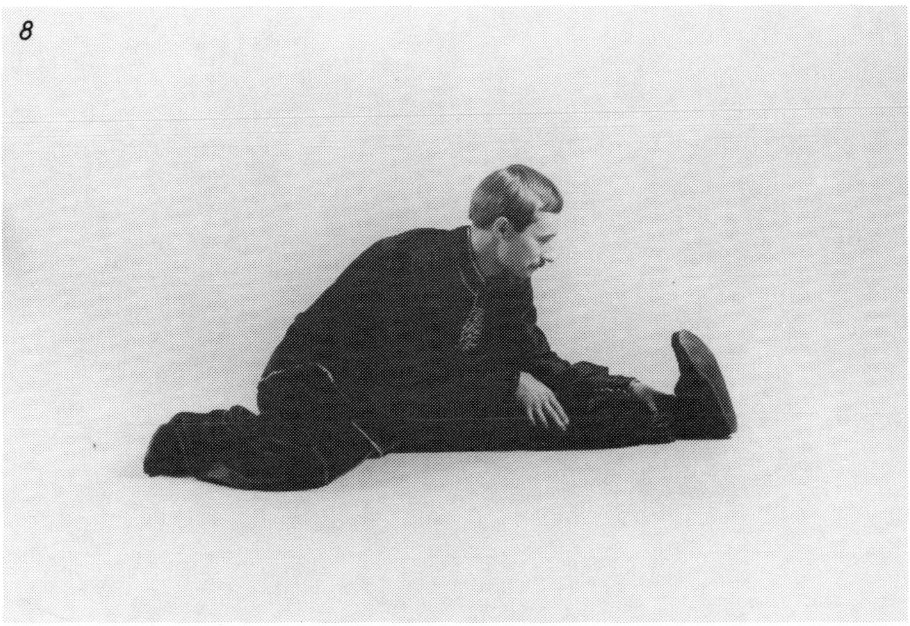

Next, grab between your knee and your ankle with your left hand.

9

Grab the instep of your left foot with both hands. Pull your foot toward you, stretching your ankle.

10

Keeping your right leg flat, touch your chin to your ankle. Hold this position for at least 30 seconds.

Back and leg stretch

1

Place both knees on the ground and both arms in front of you. Place both fists on the ground.

2

Now place your arms behind you with your hands in a fist position. Point your toes back as you move your upper body.

3

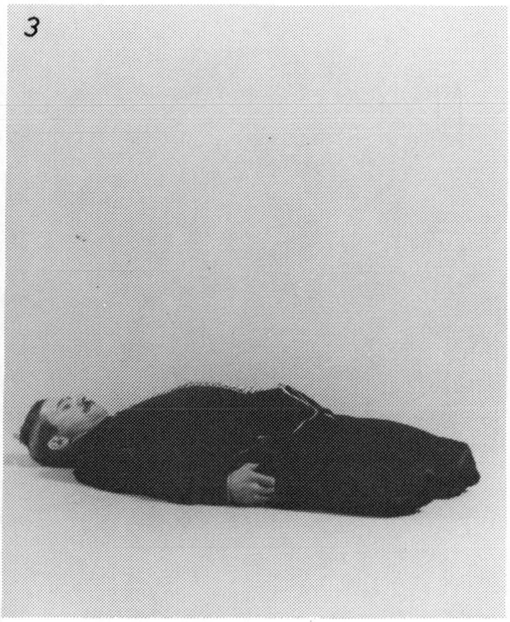

Lean your body back and lay your back flat on the ground with both arms at your sides. Keep your knees on the ground.

Behind-the-head stretch

1

Begin this stretch from a sitting position, hands at your sides and legs spread two feet apart.

2

Grab the top portion of your left foot with both hands and place it against your chest.

3

Keeping your right leg straight, place your left leg on your left shoulder.

4

From this position, pull your left leg so that your left knee is right over your shoulder. Your left hand should support your leg.

5

Keeping your balance, grab your left leg and place it behind your head. Use your right hand to hold your foot, if necessary.

Double-chin-to-toe stretch ■

From a sitting position, place your feet in front of you approximately four-to-five feet apart.

Starting with your right leg, grab just above your right knee with your right hand.

3

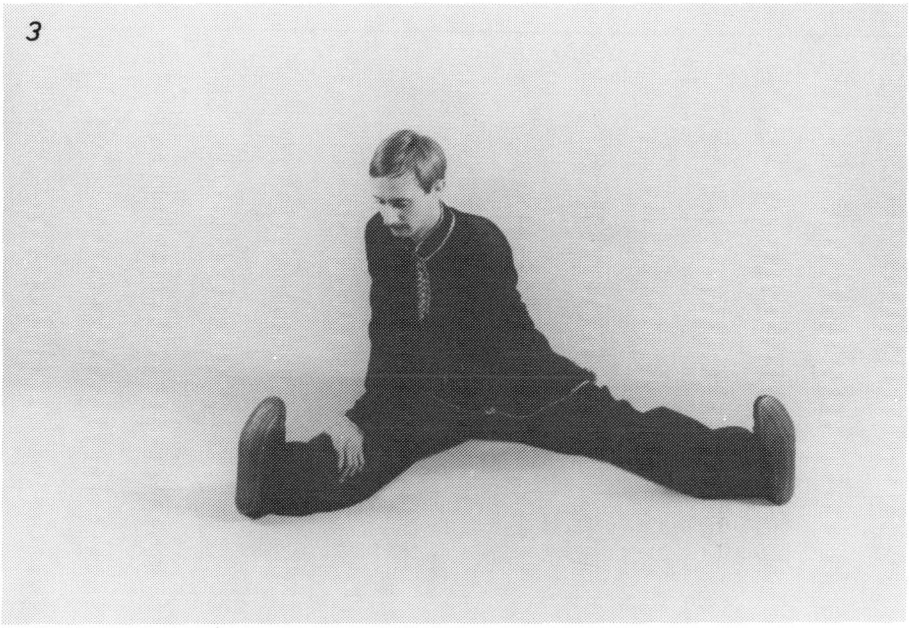

Lean your upper body toward your right side and grab your shin with your left hand.

4

Stretching even further, grab the instep of your right foot with your right hand, bending your ankle toward your body.

Keeping your right hand in place, place your left hand on your instep. Hold this position for 30 seconds.

Finally, keeping your hands on your instep, pull your upper body toward your foot and touch your chin to your toe.

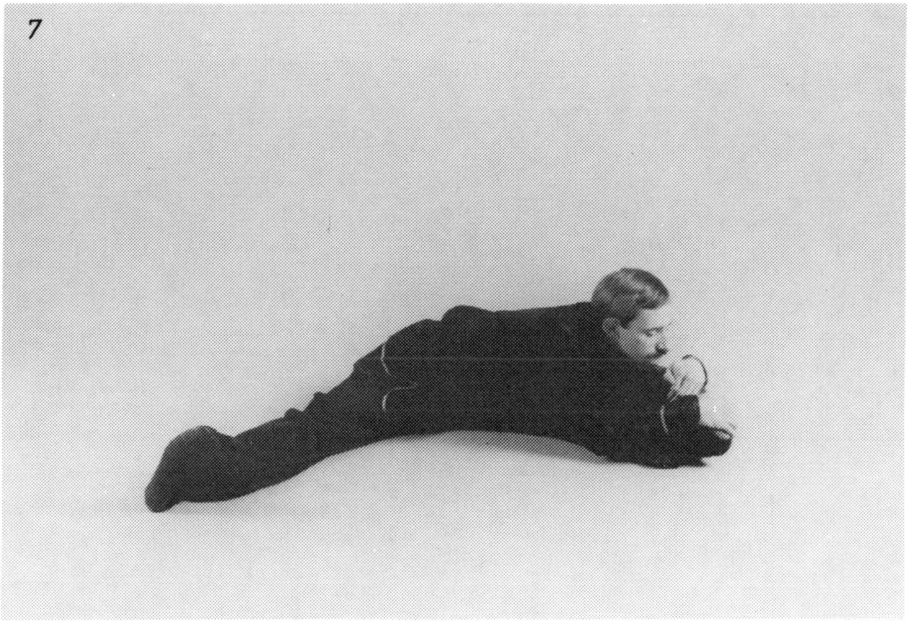

Repeat these steps for your left leg.

Leg and upper body stretch■

Place yourself on the ground in a seated position with legs together and hands on your legs.

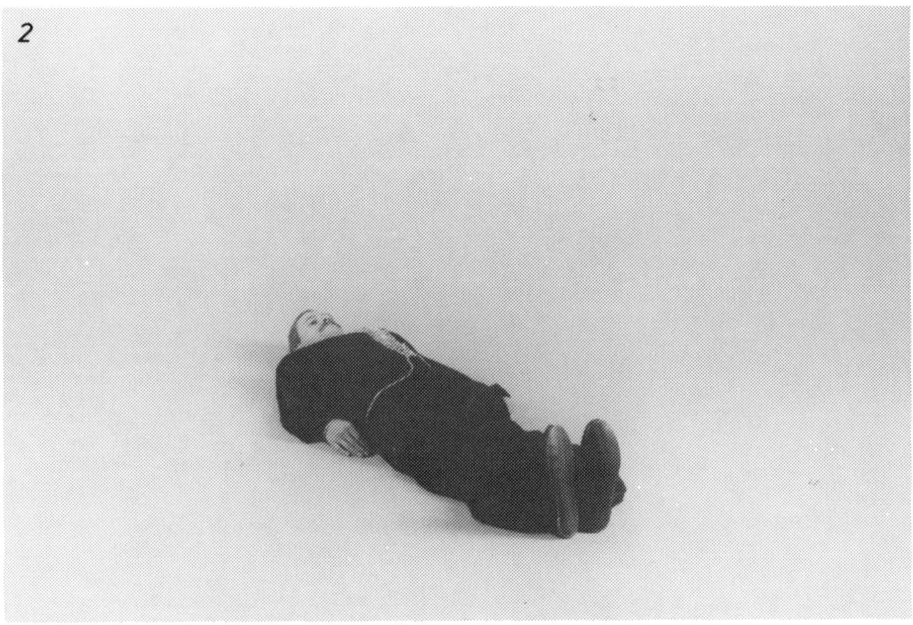

Slowly lean your body back until you are laying flat on the floor with your toes upward.

Spread your legs about three feet apart and slowly pull both legs toward your head.

Place the tips of your toes behind your head. Keep your hands flat on the ground, and most importantly, keep your back flat.

5

In this position, lean your upper body up in front of you and put both arms in the air.

6

Reach all the way out and pull your upper body past your legs. Keep your legs straight and your toes on the ground.

Leg-behind-the-head stretch

Begin this stretch from a squatting position, with both legs bent.

Grab your left upper leg with your left hand and grab your bottom ankle with your right hand. Then bend your body so your head is one inch from the ground.

Lift your left leg, and your body should roll to the ground. Place your left foot behind your head, holding your leg in place.

Straighten your right leg, place your left hand to your side and open your right hand.

Reverse leg stretch

1

With both fists resting on the ground, bend your left leg, keeping your left foot flat on the ground. Straighten your right leg and keep the toes pointing upward.

2

Keeping both fists on the ground, move your body toward your left side and then switch positions.

End up with your right leg bent and foot flat on the floor. Your left leg should be straight with toes pointed upward.

Ankle Stretching

Ankle stretching enhances your mobility by helping you more easily move around in a low posture. It also helps you lower your stances.

In monkey kung-fu, low ground techniques and kicking make up a number of the moves in the forms. Therefore, properly stretching those muscles helps you get quite low. Your opponent will have more trouble reaching such a low target. He will have to commit himself to you by reaching down to punch or kick you. Then you can easily spring up and attack.

Stretching the ankles constantly will help you do the forms with the same control but in a much lower stance.

Ankle stretches

Starting from a forward stance, place your hands on your right bended knee. Keep your back straight.

Keeping your right leg flat, push down on your right leg. This stretches your ankle.

3

Continue practicing this movement until your knee is fairly low to the ground and your foot flat.

Ankle and knee stretch

Sit flat on the floor with both legs together, toes pointed upward and both hands flat on the floor.

Next, pull your legs as close to your body as possible. Your feet should be flat together.

Lean your upper body up from this position, placing both arms in front of you with fists resting on the ground.

Pull your fists toward you and push your body forward. Feet should be together.

5

Lean your body up so that your back is completely straight with both knees flat on the ground and hands on your legs.

Back Flexibility

Back flexibility, which develops a constant flow of energy, is an important part of internal kung-fu. Proper breathing flows through the body, mainly up and down the spine.

The back must be limber, easy to move and not stiff. But the back must also be strong to execute the rolling and ground techniques. A strong back also helps you perform the sets with less pain.

Proper stretching of the back will give you more control in the rolls and somersaults. Also, you won't tire as quickly.

Back stretches

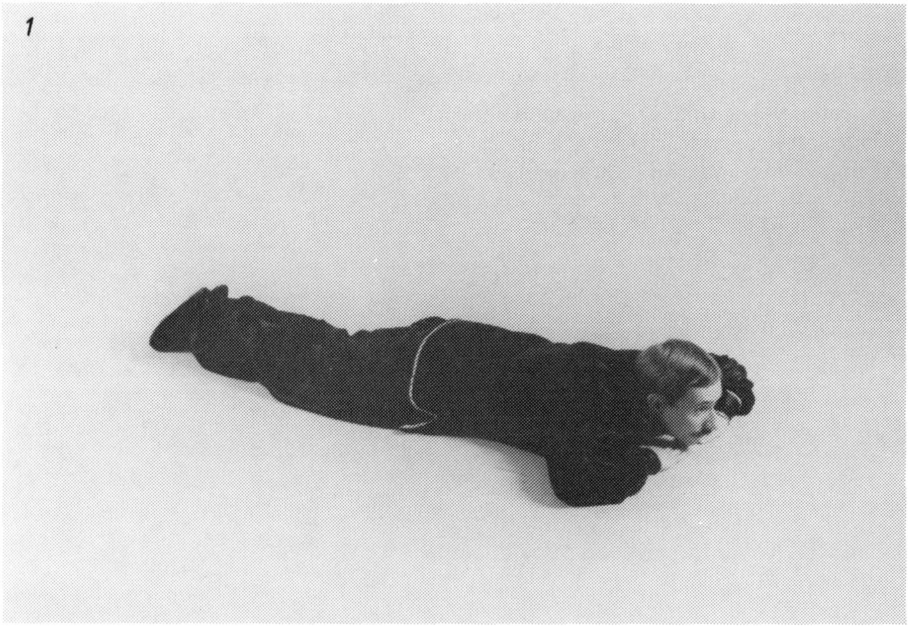

Lay flat on the floor with legs together, head up, and arms bent so your fists are flat on the ground.

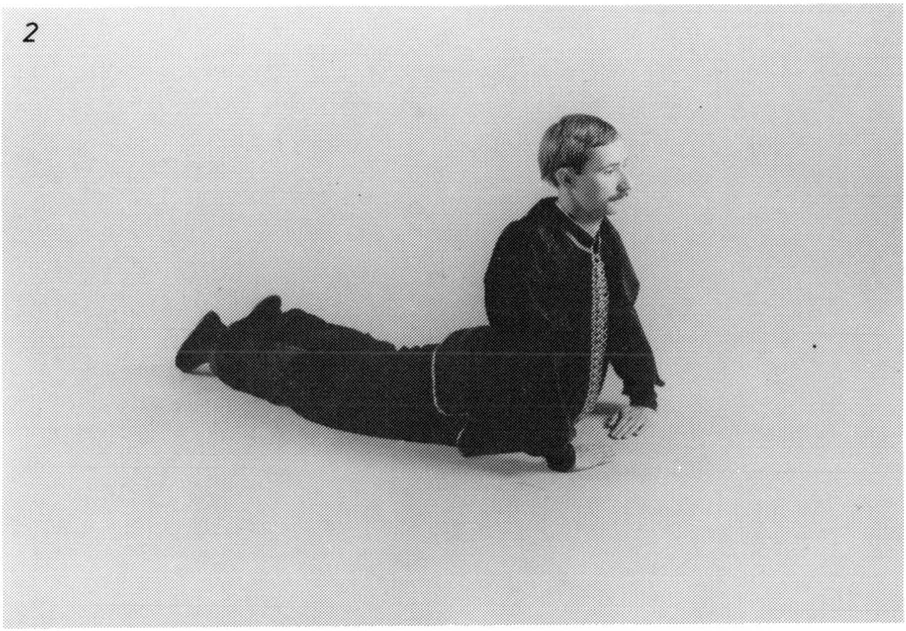

Push up with your arms until your back is straight and head is facing forward. Your legs should stay together.

Keeping your body in position, lean your head completely back and arch your back.

Straight back stretch

Place both legs on the ground, toes pointed up and arms to the side. Your fists should be on the floor.

Lift both legs and shoot them straight in front of you while balancing your body with your fists.

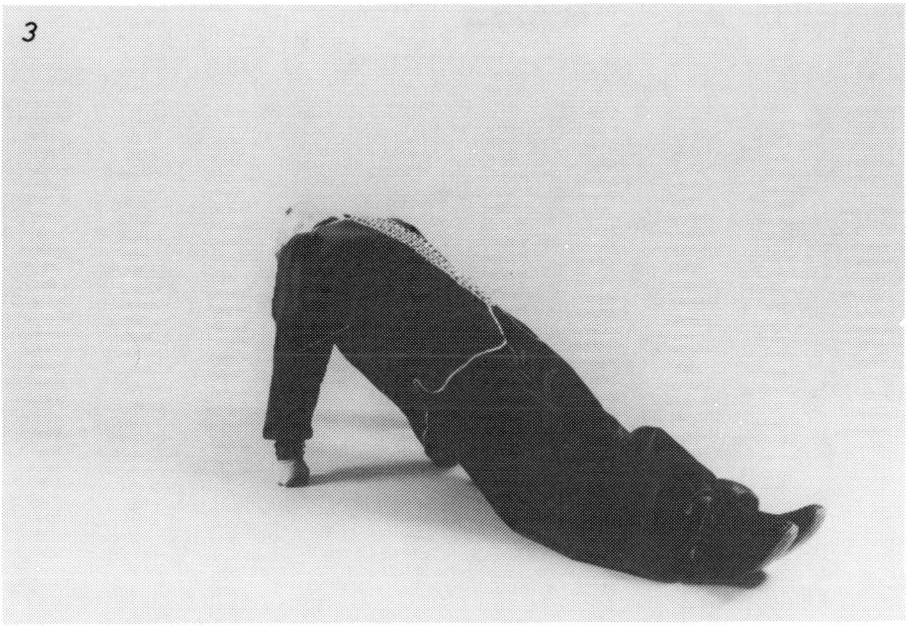

Push up your body so you are completely straight. Your head is back and your toes up.

Arched back stretch

Place both feet flat on the floor. Your back and head should also lay flat with your arms at your sides.

Your hands are pointed inward on each side of your head. Arch your back and push up with both legs and hands.

Make a complete bridge with your body, making sure the arms are straight and the toes are touching the ground.

Splits Stretching

The splits are often thought of as the most graceful pose of stretching exercises, and even as the ultimate goal of stretching. Such a unique position leaves the audience in awe.

But learning the splits is no easy task. It is perhaps the most difficult stretch to perform. It takes time — possibly years —but above all, it takes consistency of practice. Splits stretching must be done gradually, never overstretching or forcing yourself into it. You must let your body relax and adapt to the changes needed to do the splits comfortably. Above all, never be in a tremendous rush. An injury may set your stretching time back for months.

In a number of kung-fu styles, splits stretching is thought to have no meaning or purpose and is not included in the training. But splits stretching should be considered in every type of martial art, from full-contact karate and Korean forms, to traditional Chinese forms. This type of stretching allows for stronger and higher kicks, and is especially helpful for kicking styles, such as tae kwon do or hapkido. It allows your kicks to have more reach and is likely to cut down the chance of injury to your inner legs and thighs.

In tai shing pek kwar, splits stretching is a basic part of the art. Filled with ground maneuvers, leg sweeping, and splits, tai shing pek kwar could not be performed without it. The practitioner must have the limberness of a monkey who can reach for a piece of fruit with one leg and hold onto the tree with the other.

Several of the techniques used in this style incorporate the use of the splits as a means of dodging a strike, and then attacking by jumping up from a splits position while striking simultaneously.

Splits stretches

1

Begin with both legs spread approximately four-to-five feet apart, arms straight and fists flat on the ground balancing your body.

2

Slowly relax and let your body sink into a splits position with both legs and feet flat on the ground and toes pointed forward.

Lean your upper body forward until you are flat on the ground with your head looking forward.

Laying flat on the floor, lift your legs straight and keep them about three-to-four feet apart.

Keeping your knees locked, slowly spread your legs and let them fall to your sides. Point toes downward.

Pull your hands back from under you, grab your ankles and lift your head.

Front splits

Start your front splits with your left leg forward and right leg back. Keep your arms at your sides while holding your body up with your fists.

Maintaining your balance with your fists, push your left leg forward and keep your toes pointed upward.

Let your body drop so your arms no longer offer support and you are in a splits position.

Lay your upper body flat on the floor with your hands in front.

Splits change

To enhance your splits-flexibility training, face left and start from a front splits position.

Turn your body slowly until you assume a side-splits position with toes pointing forward.

Then turn your body to your right and end in a right front splits.

In one of the more advanced flexibility moves, lift your leg to your head and hold it.

Partner Stretching

Partner stretching can do wonders in helping you reach your goals. For one thing, a partner can give you that little extra push that's needed to help you reach out and stretch further. Having a person next to you will automatically stimulate more interest in and enhance any activity like stretching. Mentally, a partner gives you competition and the incentive to push a little harder. Also, it's more fun if you have someone going through the grind with you!

Several of the stretching exercises used in tai shing pek kwar require the assistance of a partner. These include the maneuvers and the extended kicking exercises.

Partner stretches

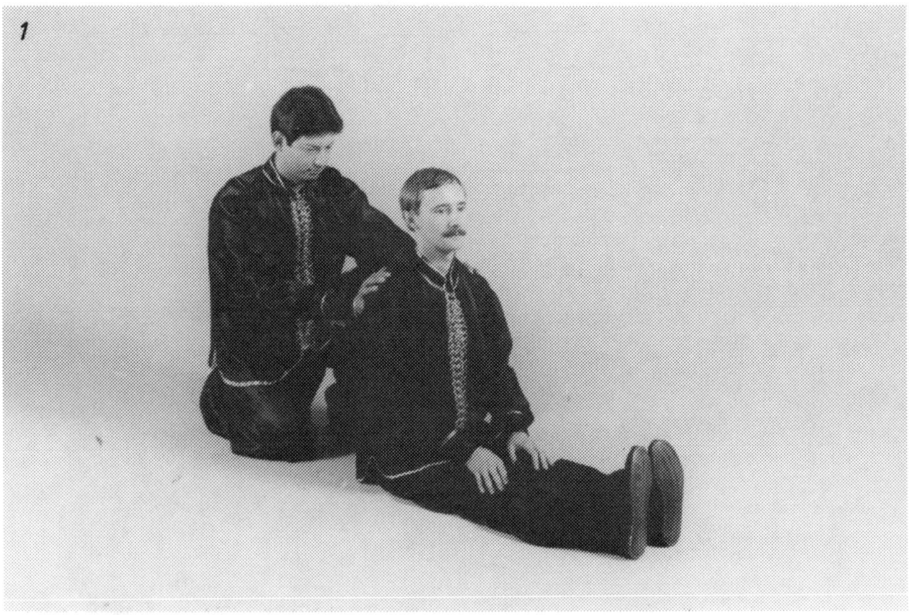

To enhance your dint-to-toe stretch, have your partner kneel behind you as you sit on the ground with both hands at your sides.

While reaching for your insteps, have your partner push you gently with both hands until you are holding both feet.

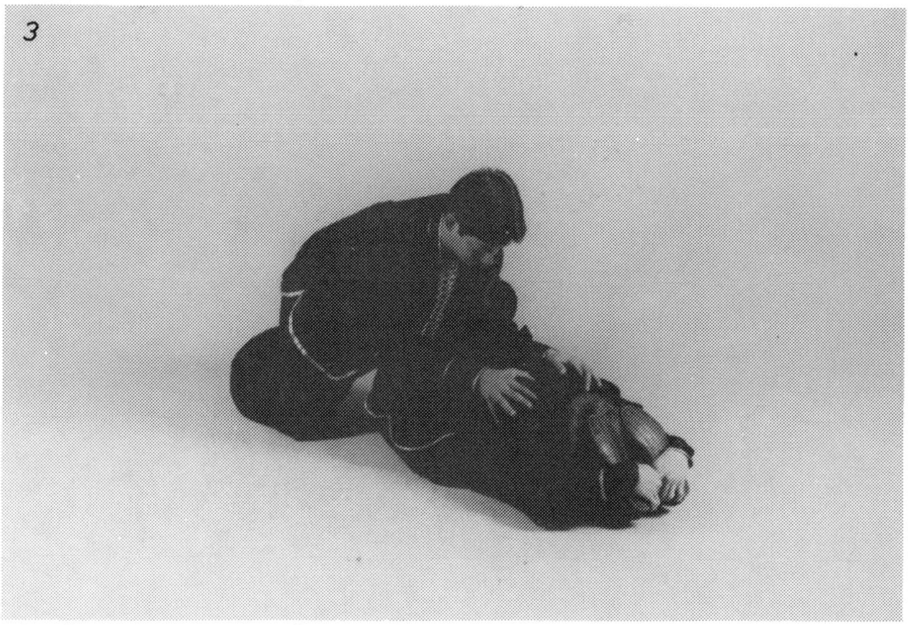

Your partner should continue pushing until you can touch your head to your toes. This exercise should be done slowly.

Partner splits stretch

1

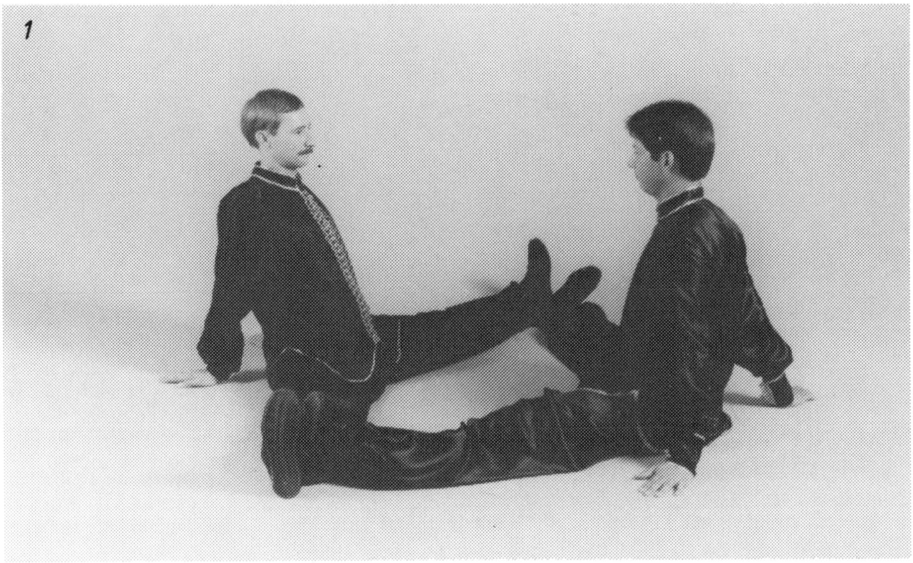

Place both you and your partner's legs together so both of you are in a semi-splits position with arms behind you.

2

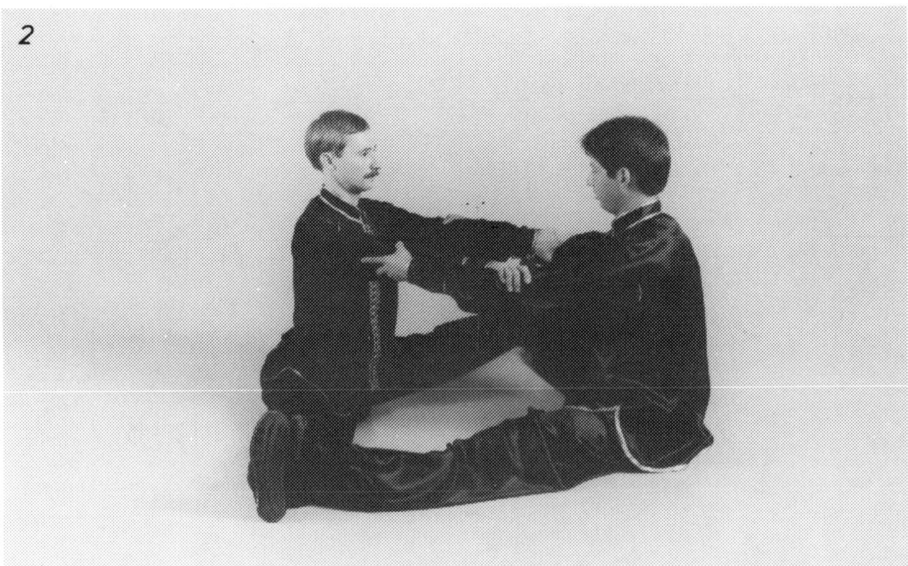

Lean forward and grab your partner's upper arm.

3

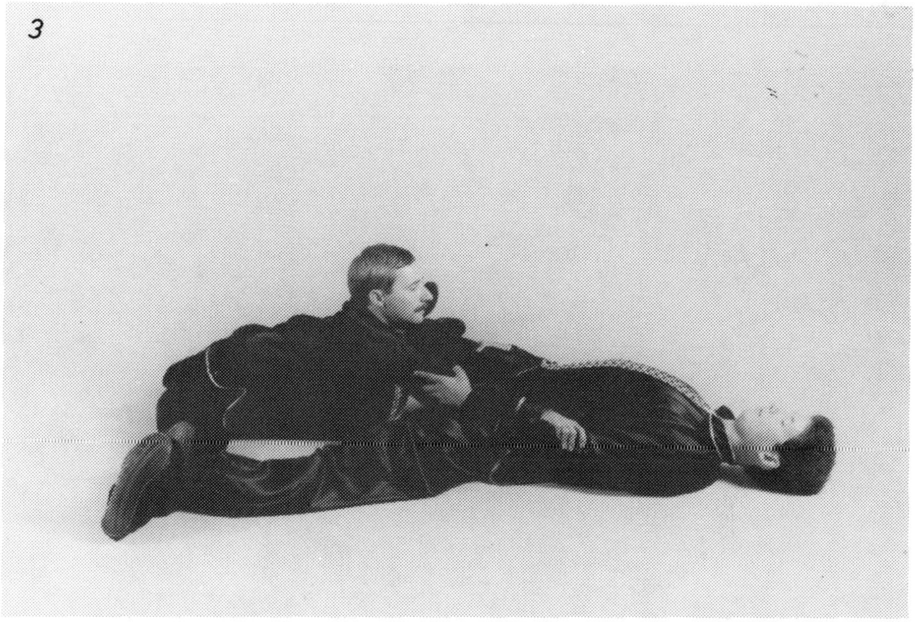

The partner on the right should slowly lean back as far as possible and pull the other to stretch his legs.

Wall stretches

Using a wall for support, lift your leg while your partner holds it behind. Keep your right leg straight.

Lower your upper body, still keeping both legs straight, as your partner slowly lifts your leg.

Front-leg splits

When a strong wall is not available, concentrate on balance as your partner holds your left leg.

As you pull up his leg, have your partner hold onto your shoulders. Keep both legs straight.

Continue gently lifting his left leg until it is straight and directly over his head.

LEARNING THE SKILLS

Learning the basics — starting from the bottom — is the only way to reach the top. For a student to become a skilled practitioner, he must learn as much as possible about the basic skills, then advance step by step.

It would be foolish to start a beginner with advanced techniques or with a form rather than the basic skills that make up the form. Without its foundation, a form has no meaning. The punches and kicks are just a set of moves, and a handful of steps and sequences do not make up an art.

Tai shing pek kwar is made up of several hundred moves and techniques. Each one of the monkey exercises, or monkey fist techniques, must be perfected to perform the movements of any of the five monkey forms.

If you make a close character study of a monkey, you'll note that he often walks with his knuckles. For this reason, several of the movements in monkey kung-fu require you to toughen your fists and knuckles by exercises such as knuckle running (running on the knuckles), or knuckle push-ups. These exercises improve your hitting ability and develop the inner stretch of the upper part of the body.

Toughening the entire body for the stone monkey form, which requires a lot of body flops, is achieved through the practice of somersaulting and ground rolling.

One of the first forms taught along with these exercises is from *tei tong* or grand earth style. This form concentrates on ground techniques such as rolling, falling and attacking from the ground. By studying this form, a student is taught to further develop his body. He gets used to the ground so that he won't be hurt when rolling and tumbling in the monkey forms.

A smooth concrete floor should be used for your practice sessions to get your body used to the floor. Then, when you begin to practice the monkey techniques, you'll be prepared.

The main advantage of ground maneuvers is that when your opponent tries to approach you and strike you while you're on the ground, he has to bend down toward you. That's when you kick and punch from the ground to his vital organs and joints.

Monkey exercises

Squat with your hands on your upper legs.

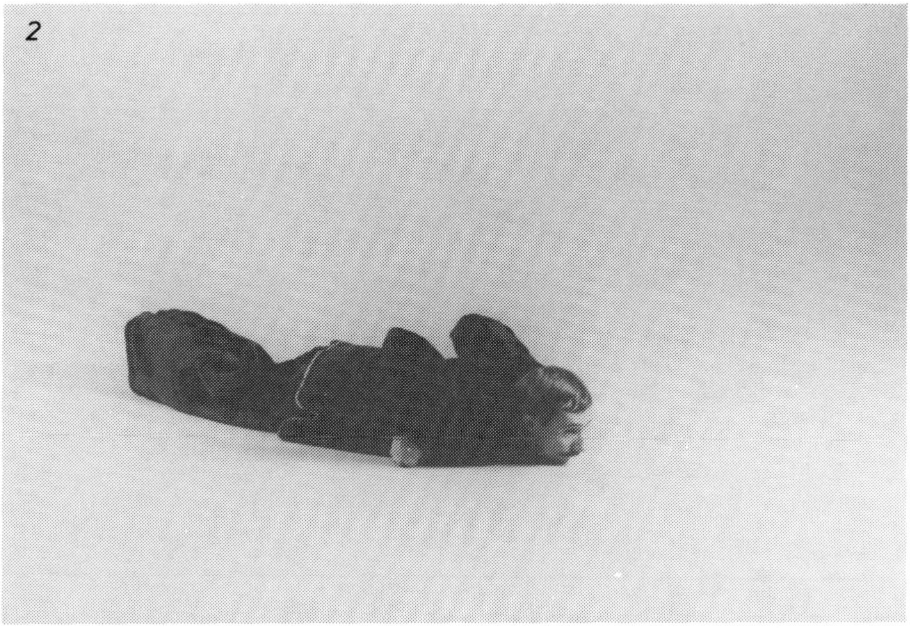

Lean forward until you are laying flat on the floor with your head up and hands in a fist position.

Lean forward, placing your arms in front and knees together.

With your fists on the ground, pull up your body. Keep your feet off the ground and knees to your chest.

Push your feet through in a kicking position, still keeping your balance with your fists.

6

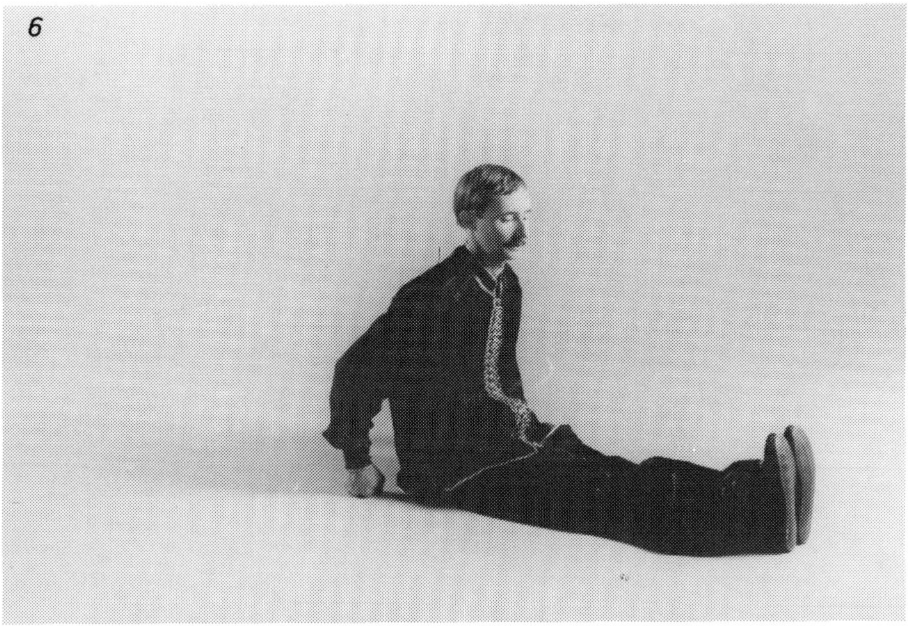

Go forward until both legs are in front and hands behind.

Pull-through walk

Begin on one side of the floor in a squatting position with both arms in front in a fist position.

Keeping your legs together, lift and pull your body forward and through.

3

With your feet off the ground, kick as you keep your legs together.

4

With your arms behind, bring both legs down and your feet flat on the ground.

Lean your body forward and lift your fists off the ground until you end in the beginning position.

Tall monkey walk

Start in a bending position with legs straight and fists on the floor.

Lean your upper body to your left and lift up your right arm.

Keeping your back straight, step forward with your right leg and lift your left arm.

Step again with your left leg. Turn your head and move with the opposite arm each time you move.

5

Switch both legs and arms as you walk across the floor.

Small monkey walk

Spread your legs, make fists and keep both arms in front. Your head is up.

Lean down to your left side and place your right hand behind. Your head is up.

Strike across with your left arm and bend your legs. Your left leg is on the ground and your arm is back.

Step forward with your left leg and begin to swing back your left arm.

5

Swing your right arm across with your head forward. Continue across the floor.

Universal monkey walk

Begin from a very low position, with the left arm back and right arm and both legs bent.

Keeping your hands in position, bring your left leg up and forward.

Continue forward with your left leg until it is on the ground. Make sure to switch legs.

Pull-through walk-across

Bend your legs with both hands in a clenched position and your right leg back.

Bring your right leg forward until your feet are together and hands in front.

Push both legs through your arms, keeping your body balanced and your arms straight.

Kicking your leg through, push your legs straight and over your head.

With your legs together, bring them in front of you.

Place your arms in front and start the pull-through again.

Cross-over push-ups

Stand with legs together and arms straight out.

Lean forward as you begin your descent. Keep arms still in front of you.

3

Hit the ground first with both arms. Your head should be up.

4

Your body should now be in a push-up position with your arms about two feet apart.

Push both legs in the air and cross them.

Land in a crossed push-up position with one leg over the other.

7

Push out again and cross your legs in the air.

8

Land in your push-up position. Start over.

Double cross-over

Start in a push-up position with arms about two feet apart.

Push up and cross your arms and legs.

3

Land with one leg over each other and one arm over the other.

4

Push up again and switch your legs and arms in the air. You should land in a regular push-up.

Back push-up

Place your arms and feet together in front of you.

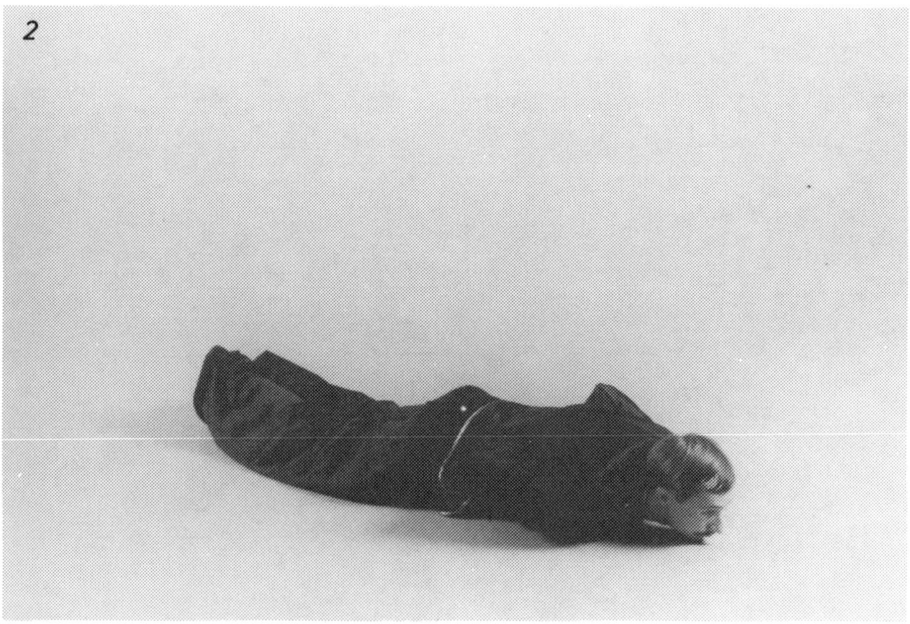

Push your body forward toward your hands, keeping your body straight and one inch off the ground.

Push your body forward until your back is straight and head is up.

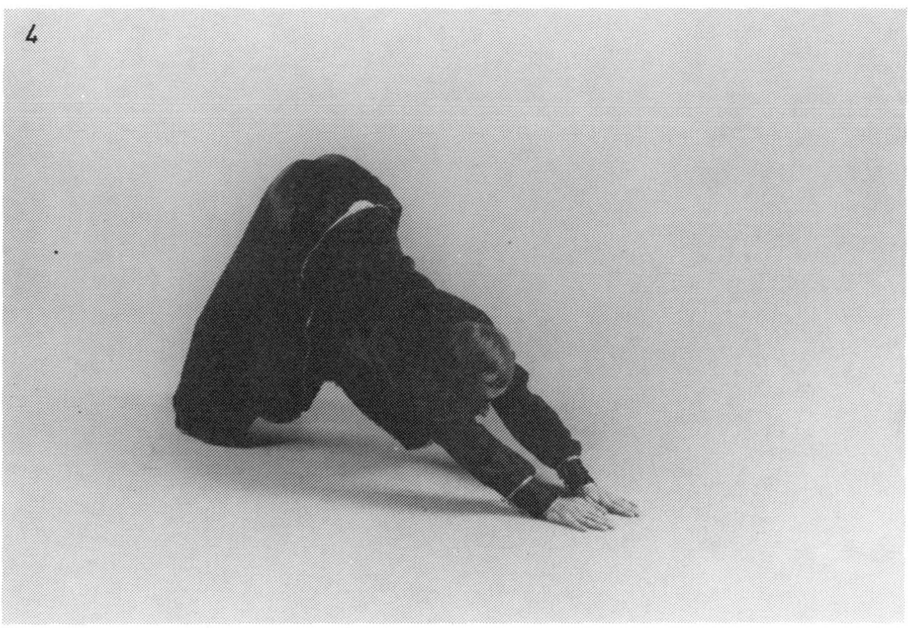

Push your body into the original position and repeat ten times.

Sitting cross-over

1

Start with your right leg bent and your left leg under your right in between the knee.

2

Kick out your left leg. Keep your right foot flat on the ground.

3

Place your left leg on top of your right upper leg. Repeat several times.

CHI KUNG: INTERNAL BREATHING

Throughout time, extraordinary feats of strength have proved that man is capable of exerting power and energy far beyond what is considered normal. This special, incredible power is referred to by most martial artists as chi, or chi kung.

This chi kung power is cultivated through the practice of proper internal breathing. Proper breathing sends the flow of energy that chi kung provides through the body wherever the energy is projected. This type of internal nourishment is gained through deep meditation while breathing in the two cycles illustrated in this book. True internal breathing training and exercises are not openly available in the average commercial martial art school. These rare skills are usually passed on to only close friends and family members.

There are two types of basic breathing postures used for meditation and cultivation of chi kung in tai shing pek kwar: the folded leg sitting posture and the straight leg sitting posture.

The Folded Leg Sitting Posture

Assume a sitting posture. The breath comes in through the nose, up the top of the head, down the spinal cord, and around the *dan tien* (abdominal area), then up through the body and out the nostrils.

The Straight Leg Sitting Posture

Start by relaxing in this posture. The breath flows through the nose, up to the head, back along the spinal cord, to the back of the legs, to the heels and up to the toes. It then turns and goes back along the top of the legs to the *dan tien*, then up the body and back through the bones.

Internal power/Chi kung

These movements should be done slowly. Start from a low front horse position.

Lean into a monkey horse with both hands cupped as your left arm circles out.

Return to your original position.

Start your second breathing exercise from the same low front horse position.

5

Lean into a monkey horse, and circle your arms with your left arm going first.

6

Lean forward with your right knee close to the ground. Begin circling your right arm.

7

Swing your right arm forward and your left arm back.

8

Pull yourself into a front horse position.

9

Finish in a front horse with both arms back. Hands should always be cupped.

MONKEY STANCES

The frightened little monkey hurriedly runs through the forest from his attacker. Suddenly, the scared young animal stops, sits down and picks a flea from his head. As his attacker rushes up, the monkey jumps high in the air and knocks his opponent down with continuous strikes. He then hurriedly flees.

Monkey stances or postures — unlike many of the conventional kung-fu stances — give the opponent no chance to engage in the guessing game of "what's his next angle of attack?" Each movement of the monkey must be sudden, instantaneous and without warning. Just as the monkey is sly and tricky, his posture must equally be deceiving. He is unpredictable, elusive, and deceptive — giving no advanced warning of his intentions. His eyes say one thing, his body does another. Seemingly tucked into a ball, the monkey must be able to spring out and attack. Such a feat requires a high degree of balance, flexibility, and strength to be effective.

Making a character study of a monkey standing or walking is a must, but character studies alone don't do the job. Learning to become a monkey — rather than just act like one — requires an elusive mental attitude or spirit few people can cultivate.

Monkey stances

1

The tall monkey stance is sometimes rather high with one leg slightly bent and body back.

2

Moving from a tall monkey position requires more bending of the knees.

3

Another tall stance, characteristic of both the tall and wooden monkey, is the moving back stance. The body is back and the arms are close.

4

A show of fear would signify the wooden monkey.

5

The drunken monkey starts in a relatively high horse with both hands near the chest.

6

Slowly, the drunken monkey slumps to a bent, two-fisted position.

7

Another stance characteristic of most monkey forms is the bent leg stance, with one leg straight and the other bent and held with one hand.

8

The stone monkey focuses on drop-type stances usually from a retreating position.

Drop on both knees with arms keeping guard.

Both lost and wooden also share this next position. A defense is prepared.

For no reason but distraction, the monkey brings his hands together and mimics eating a flea plucked from his head.

Monkey stances must be done very quickly and unpredictably at the outset of an attack.

13

Retreat from the attack.

14

Turning back, attack once the opponent has committed himself.

15

Each monkey technique is based on the proper stance. Start from a low basic horse, feet forward and arms at the sides.

16

Step to one side and look at your opponent.

Step into a blocking position.

Step to another position and strike.

Keep both hands ready for attack.

Drop to a low, unreachable target. Bring the opponent to you.

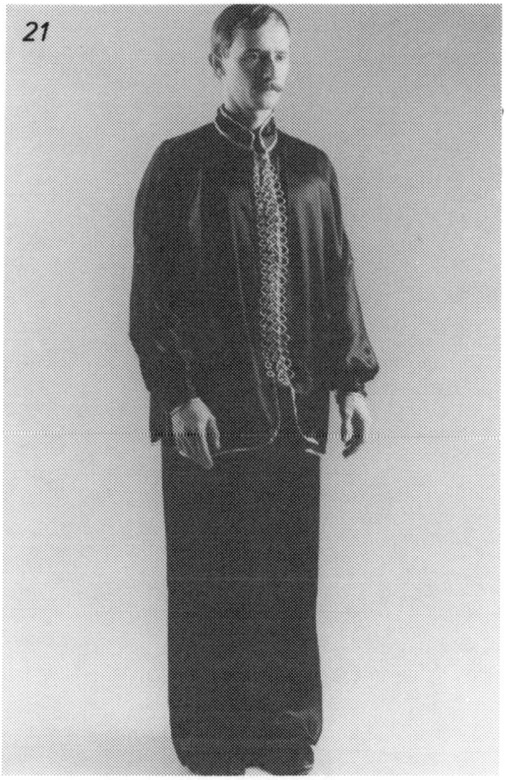

All monkeys begin their movements from the basic standing position.

Blocking down and hard with the knee is stressed in the stone monkey.

Switch to the opposite side.

Being flexible is the key to every monkey movement. The twist-over position begins from a low, strong horse stance.

Looking to your right, block the attack with your right arm.

Continually blocking, turn around and face the opposite direction.

Keeping your right leg bent, twist and straighten your left leg.

Lift your left leg into a kicking position. Grab your opponent and pull him toward your kick.

Monkey kicks

1

One such variety is the high front-kick from the right or left front stance with hands out to the side.

2

Pull up your knee, then snap it to the head. Keep your back heel flat.

3

Another classical move is the crescent kick which begins from a forward stance.

4

Keeping your back leg straight, lift your left leg and move it in a circular motion.

5

Strike to your opponent's head.

6

The monkey back kick is done from a low position. Hands should be placed on your knees.

7

Hit the ground with both fists. Look behind you and bring your knees close to the ground.

8

Push out to a back kick. Your arms should help maintain balance.

Monkey front kick

The monkey front kick starts from a low, scissors-type position with the right leg back.

Lift your body slightly, bringing up your right leg.

Keeping balance with your left leg, perform a right front kick and block with your left hand.

Lower your right leg and grab with both hands.

Start from a low, crossed monkey position with your left leg on top of your right.

Recoil to the original position, while looking the opposite way.

Shoot to a left side kick and look in the direction of the kick.

Double side kick

Start from a low squatting position with knees bent, feet flat on the floor and hands on each knee.

Looking toward your opponent, lean to your right with both fists on the ground.

Bring up your left arm, fist clenched in a blocking position.

Lift your body. Knees should be tucked with the weight on your right arm.

5

With legs together, strike your opponent with a straight kick.

Side kick

1

Place your right fist on the ground and bring up your left arm in a blocking position.

2

Like all monkey maneuvers, start with the basic low monkey squatting position.

3

Bring your left leg close to your chest, then kick toward your left while keeping balance with your right arm and leg.

Ground roll kick

1

Start in a low monkey stance position with both feet on the floor and hands in close.

2

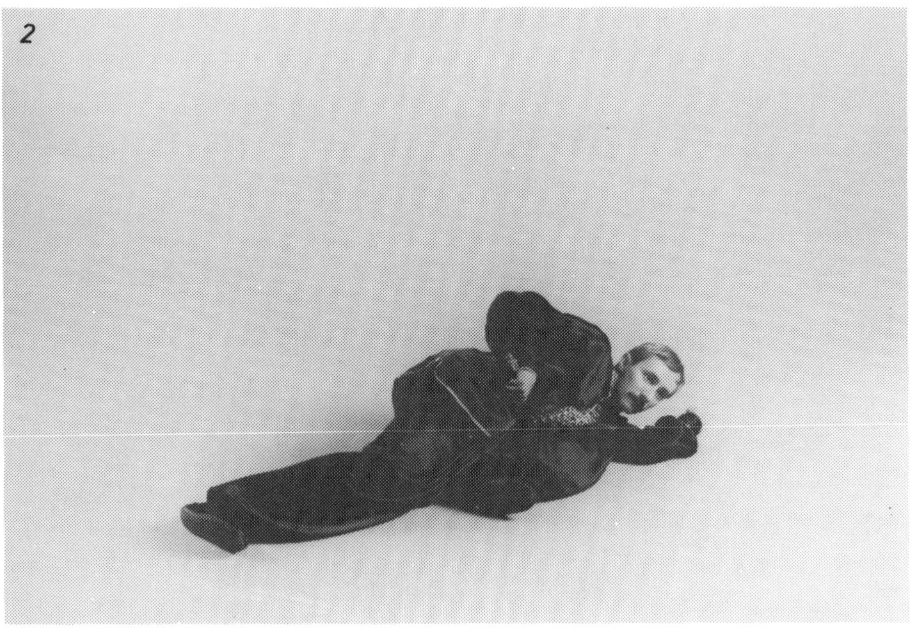

Fall to your left side with your right leg straight, left arm on the ground and left leg bent.

With your left leg on the ground, move your leg in a circular motion.

As you circle your left leg, keep your right leg straight. Your foot should now be at your head.

5

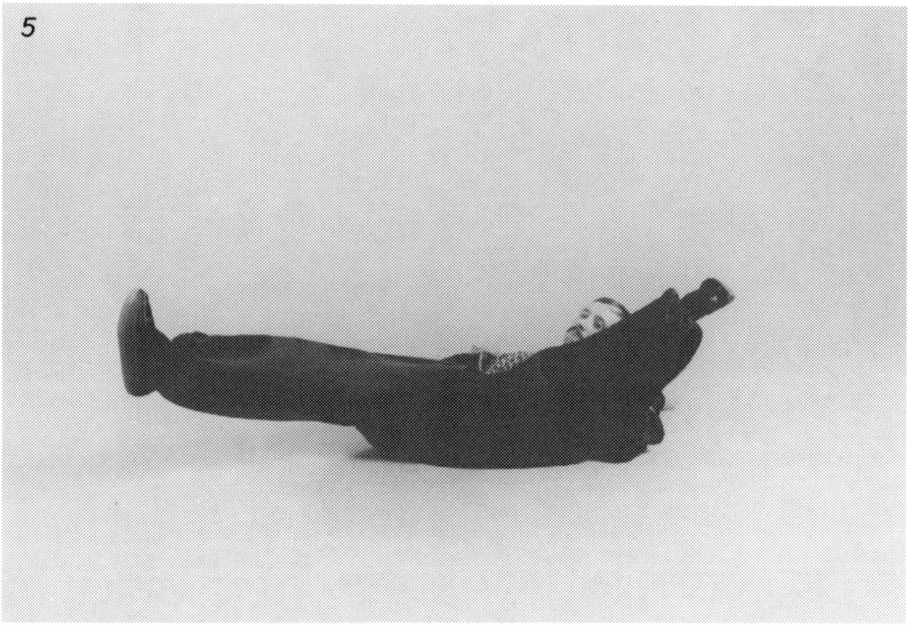

As your right leg gets closer to your original position, your left leg should straighten and begin its circular movements.

6

Your right leg is flat on the ground as your left leg circles your head.

7

As you land your left leg, the left foot should be flat on the ground and the arms in a blocking position.

Falling side kick

1

Characteristic of the wooden and lost monkey, you should be in a low position with left leg out and back leg bent.

2

As you fall, cock your left leg and form a block with your arms.

3

As your opponent approaches, strike with a side kick.

Back leg kick

1

Lean on the right side of your back and look toward your left. Your right fist is on the ground.

2

Block up with your left arm.

Push out your right leg behind and slightly lift your body.

Reach a full extension of your left leg.

THE STONE MONKEY

The leader or strongest of the monkeys is the stone monkey. This monkey is tough, like a strong bully, playfully being able to dish it out and take it.

The stone monkey is the hardest form to perfect. Its mastery requires that considerable time be spent toughening and hardening the body. Techniques in which the practitioner lands on the elbow and knee joints require even more practice time.

This form is primarily an external form relying on physical power and strength. It is well-suited to a muscular or strong person who can use force against force, is resilient to blows, and like a rock, is impervious to pain.

Training for this form should be done on smooth concrete. Much time must be spent running on the knuckles to toughen them and somersaulting to toughen the back.

The Stone Monkey

Your opponent steps up and grabs you by the arm.

You bring your left hand around and grab the top of his arm.

With this grip, draw him off balance by pulling his arm toward the ground.

Lift your right leg.

Kick your attacker's front leg.

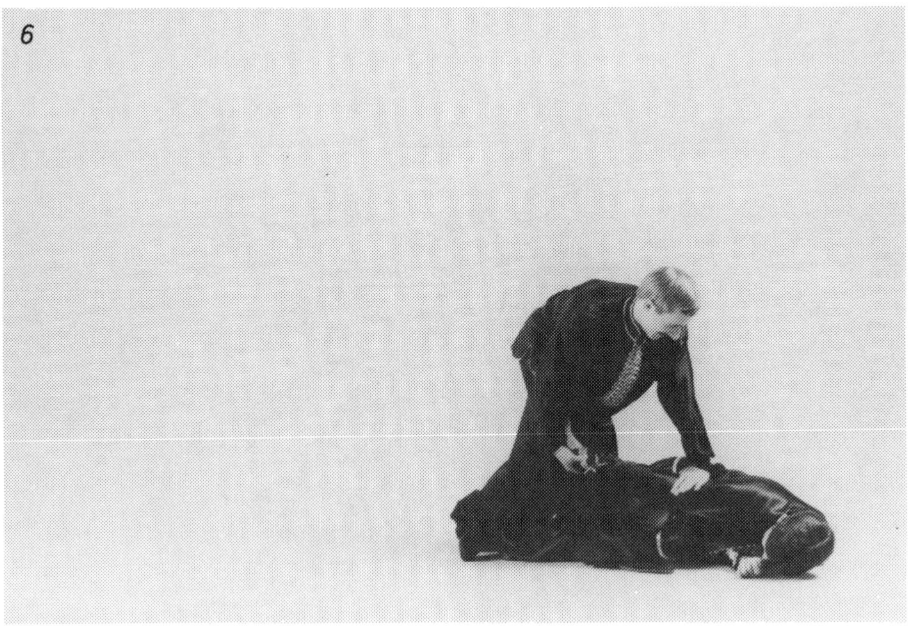

Push as you kick. The opponent will fall.

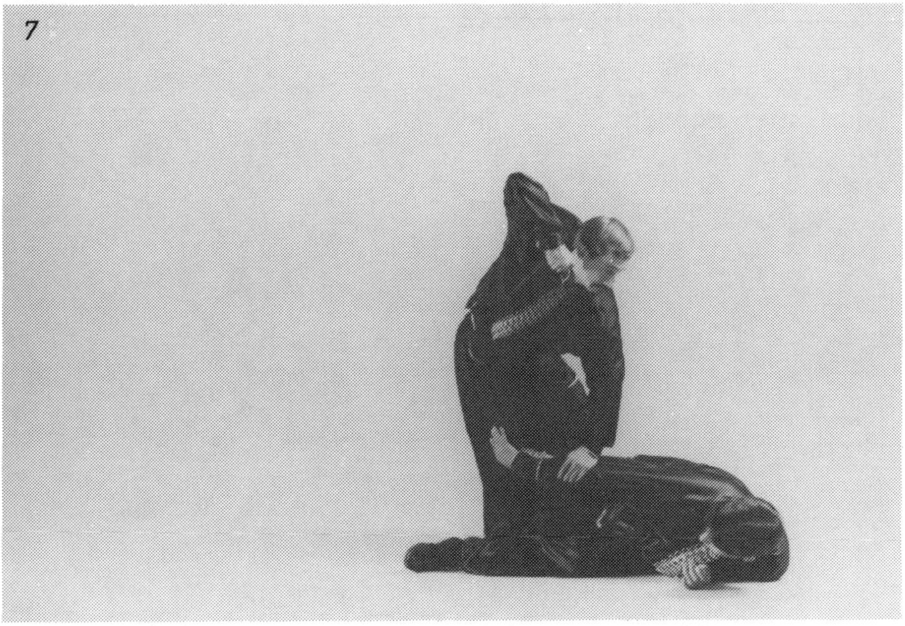

Step in and prepare for a right-arm strike.

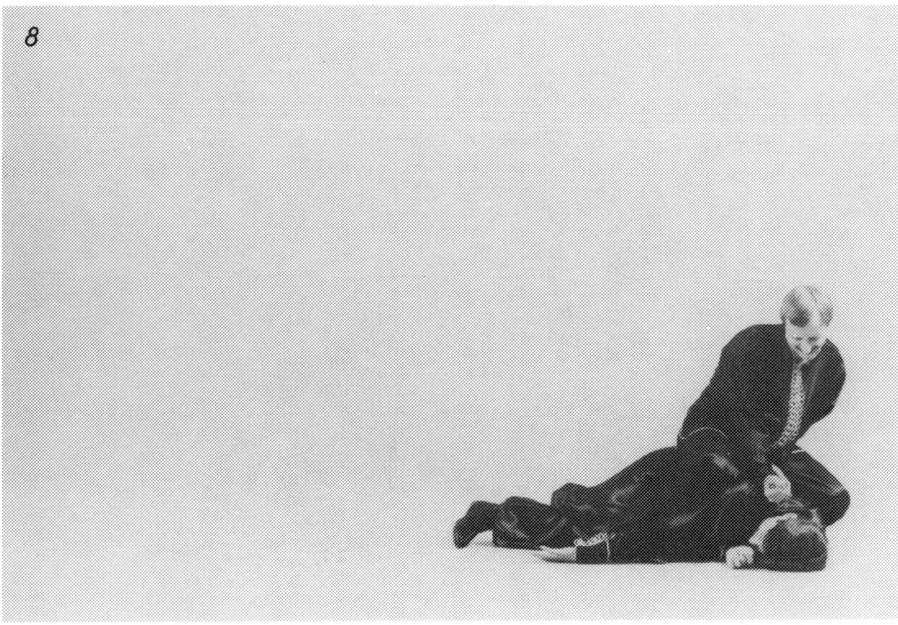

Climb across your fallen opponent and strike to his head with your fist.

Second stone monkey

Begin with knees slightly bent.

Pull back your left leg as your opponent begins to attempt a sweep.

Jump high to avoid your attacker's sweep.

Land on your opponent, breaking his right leg at the knee.

Add a strike to the head.

Strike again with your right hand.

THE DRUNKEN MONKEY

When it comes to food, monkeys aren't too discriminating. They'll eat anything. Strolling into a nearby village, a band of monkeys would frequently steal a few bottles of wine, and in some cases, even got drunk.

A monkey who has overindulged in wine is full of awkward and strange movements. Looking sick and feeling worse, the monkey falls and stumbles as he walks. A monkey in this state looks like easy prey.

The drunken monkey form is a spiritual form. The practitioner becomes *spiritually* drunk, rather than physically drunk. His movements are jagged and twisted and seemingly off balance. Yet he is in total control.

Moving in a broken rhythm pattern, the stylist must rely on his internal power to successfully attack from an off-balance position. In each stumble and fall, the practitioner is still able to defend himself. For instance, when the monkey falls on his back, he kicks his opponent at the same time.

The drunken monkey form requires a high degree of

flexibility. The monkey will stick one foot behind his head, or hop around on one leg.

In other drunken forms, the practitioner shows a certain degree of back flexibility. But a drunk monkey does not bend in the same manner as a man. He has the odd, flexible movements of a monkey.

Drunken monkey

As your opponent prepares for an attack, the drunken monkey gives the impression of being completely off balance and vulnerable.

As you are being attacked, slump to the ground when you see his side kick.

Fall to the ground as your opponent closes.

As he strikes, kick his punch up and add another kick to his groin.

When the groin kick connects, he will fall toward you.

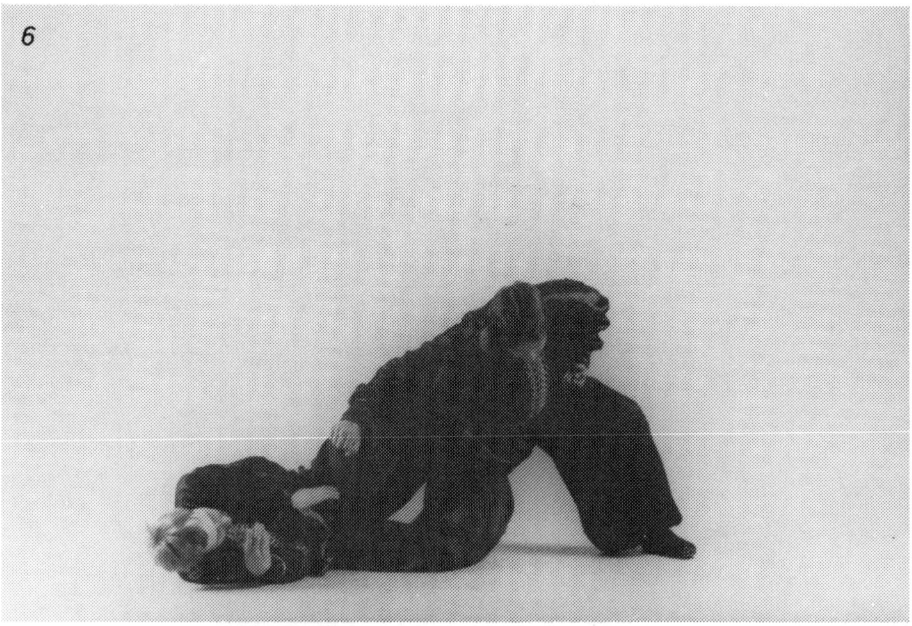

Finish with a kick to his head.

Drunken monkey

You are in an awkward and off-balance low position as your attacker begins to kick.

As he starts to kick, guide his striking foot away with your left hand.

Avoid contact by falling to the ground as he executes his side kick.

Lift your left leg and strike him with a kick.

5

Use both legs to strike his groin area.

Drunken monkey

As you weave, your opponent pushes to take advantage of your apparent drunken position.

Immediately slump to a low position as he starts his kick.

Blocking his kick with your left hand, pull back with your right hand.

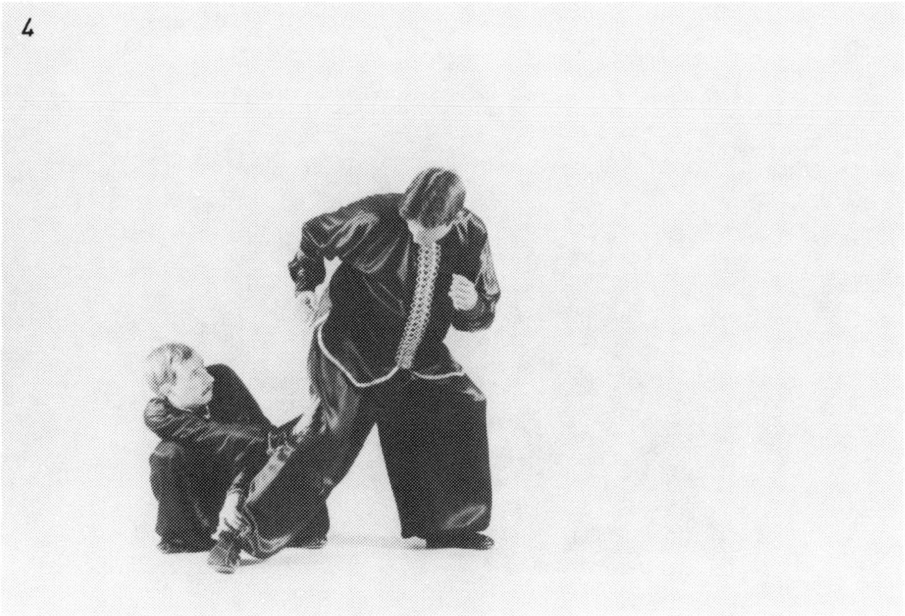

Hit the back of his right leg with a palm strike.

5

As your opponent tries to strike again, grab his right arm.

6

Twist his right arm, and pull out your left arm in preparation for a strike.

Finish with an elbow strike to his head.

Second drunken monkey ■

As your opponent squares off, creep toward the ground while wearing a sickly look on your face.

Simulate passing out and lean back as your opponent begins to attack.

As he lunges for an attack, continue to roll back and kick his arm.

Then kick his knee to further eliminate any danger.

THE WOODEN MONKEY

The wooden monkey is smart and clever, perhaps more so than the other monkeys. He is always able to outwit his opponent. Using his brain rather than just his brawn, he takes advantage of his enemy's commitment to attack. For instance, the wooden monkey will lead his enemy to chase him. As soon as his enemy commits himself to the chase and gets close enough, the monkey turns around and attacks. Since the opponent is committed, his defenses are down and he is completely open for a blow to any of his vulnerable areas.

The wooden monkey relies on mental concentration, trying to make his opponent believe he's going to use one technique, then doing another. This set depends on the power of *illusion*.

The monkey is extremely aggressive and relentless in his attack, never knowing the word fear. He is always looking for an opening in his opponent's defenses. His attacks come from several different directions when least expected.

Wooden monkey

As the attacker readies his strike, step back in a scissors position.

When his punch comes toward you, block up with your left arm while maintaining balance with your right arm.

Completely turn your position around with both fists on the ground and bring up your right leg.

Then push out toward your opponent and kick his front leg.

Knock him to the ground.

Second wooden monkey

Start from a low horse stance as your attacker begins his move.

Block up with your left hand as your attacker lunges forward with a right punch.

3

Turn down to your left, pivoting on your knee. Turn and swing with your right leg.

4

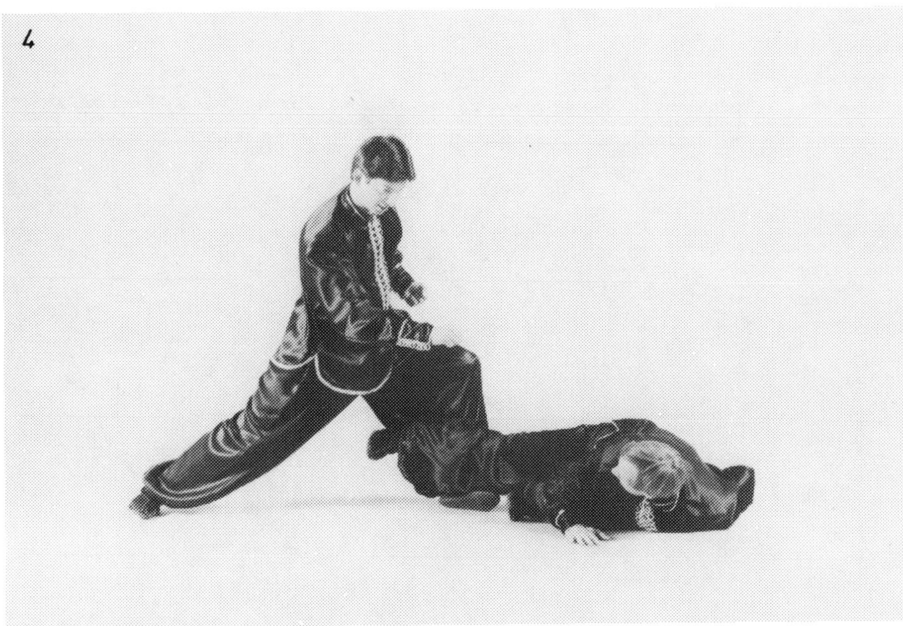

Continue spinning your leg, keeping balance with your hands as you hit the inside of his leg.

5

Follow through and you knock down your opponent.

Third wooden monkey

1

Begin in a low position, balancing yourself with your right arm.

2

As you are being attacked, block up with your left arm.

Turn completely around to face your opponent. Pull back your right leg.

Kick as his front left leg comes forward.

Break his left leg as you knock him back.

THE TALL MONKEY

The tall monkey form shows the movements of a tall monkey with long arms and legs. Staying just outside of his opponent's reach, the tall monkey hits the opponent in the face and laughs. Appearing to be tucked into a ball, the tall monkey can jump out and use his length to attack an opponent farther away.

The tall monkey form is an aggressive form, characterized by low stances and continuous circular arm swings. However, it does not have as many ground maneuvers as the other monkey forms.

This method of long-arm fighting is ideal for tall students who can easily capitalize on their reach. Though a small person could do the movements of the tall monkey, it is more suited for a tall person.

Tall monkey

The tall monkey techniques are performed from a slightly higher position and feature the knees bent.

As your opponent lunges with a front punch, slightly bend down your body to avoid the punch.

3

As soon as you avoid his strike, immediately apply a left crescent kick to the face.

4

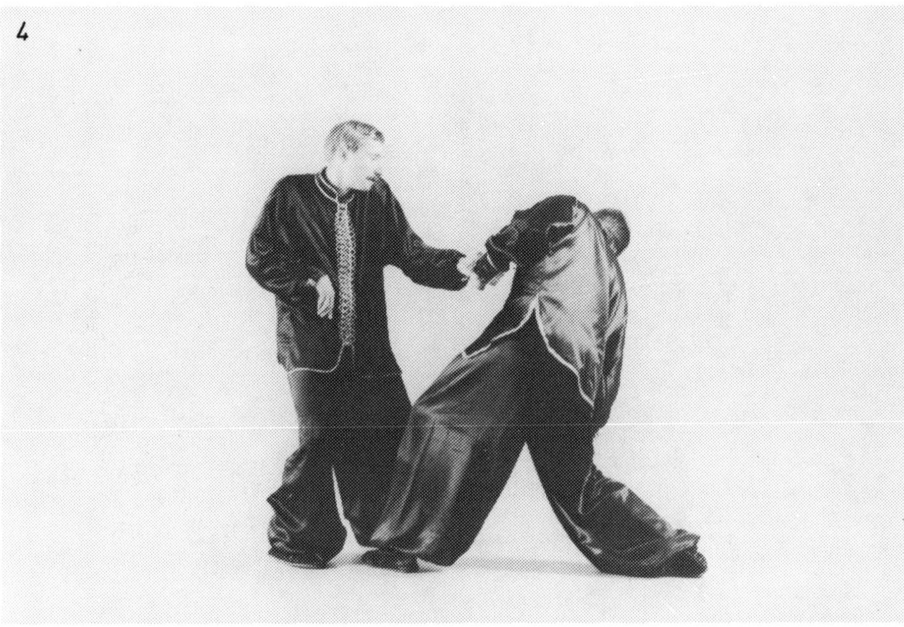

Reach out and grab his left arm by the wrist.

5

Pulling his arm toward you, deliver a right leg roundhouse kick.

6

Pull back from your kick, and deliver a blow to the back of his knee.

Second tall monkey

Start in a low squatting position. Lean slightly back and look at your on-coming opponent.

As your opponent moves in for an attack, pull up your arms to prepare for his maneuver.

As he strikes toward your head, counter with a right fist to your opponent's elbow.

Immediately lean back on your left fist and pull your right leg into a kicking position.

5

Execute a monkey side kick to your attacker's abdomen, all the while keeping his right arm out of attack range.

6

After knocking him to the ground, quickly lean toward him to strike.

7

Stepping in, strike to the head.

THE LOST MONKEY

The lost monkey form is like a monkey who has lost his way and has become frightened of all the noises around him. But after being left alone for awhile, he suddenly becomes very angry.

This monkey form is characterized by the practitioner's look of innocence and confusion, which is indeed a fraud. His feet and hand movements are extremely quick. By changing his footwork continually, he makes his moves hard to follow. The lost monkey form requires agility and more flexibility than the other monkey forms.

Though the movements in this form are subtle and hard to understand, each has a self-defense application.

Lost monkey

The lost monkey techniques give the appearance of the defender being afraid and confused. In this position, he looks up to his attacker.

As your opponent lifts his leg for a kick, lean back and guard your face.

As he lunges forward with a front kick, balance yourself with your left fist and block up while grabbing his leg.

Close in on your opponent and begin kicking with your left leg.

Pushing back his front leg, kick his other leg.

Knock him to the ground, keeping his front leg away from you.

Jump extremely high over your opponent, bringing your legs together.

Aim to land both feet on his chest.

9

The impact breaks his ribs and chest.

Second lost monkey

Lean in a low squatting position as you face your opponent.

As he attacks, step back in a confused motion while watching his attacking right punch.

Reach out and grab your opponent's arm.

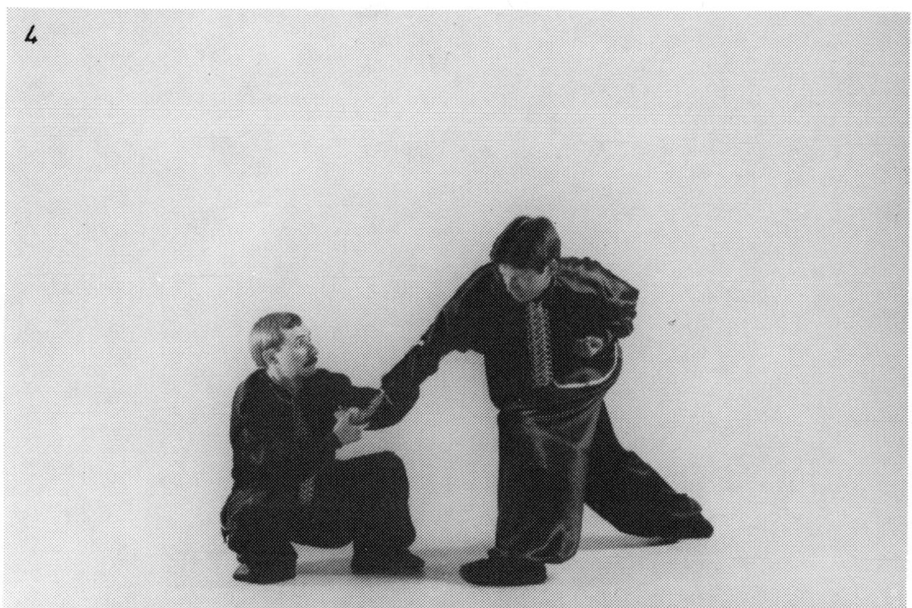

Pull your opponent off balance using his forward motion.

Pull him down until you hear his fist hit the ground.

Strike his head with your left elbow.

MONKEY WEAPONS

Unlike the classical Chinese kung-fu styles, in which the weapon techniques bear little relationship to the style as a whole, tai shing pek kwar weapon techniques stem directly from the monkey's use of a weapon.

For instance, tiger style kung-fu is a strong external style, using strong claw-hand techniques like a tiger's claw to pull and grab. However, it would be difficult for a tiger to use a stick or spear. So the masters of the tiger style incorporated other weapon techniques into the system.

But since a monkey has two arms with which to strike, and two hind legs with which to walk, a human practitioner can adapt a monkey's style of swinging and hitting with a stick or staff.

The Staff

The staff, considered a conventional weapon, is probably the most effective and well-known form of weapon in monkey kung-fu. Kou Sze learned the staff form while observing several monkeys playing outside the prison window of his cell. He noticed that one of the monkeys picked up a long stick, similar in size to a staff. The monkey walked around with the staff on his shoulder, playfully swinging and twirling it around. Kou Sze was fascinated by the monkey's playful antics with the stick. So impressed was he that he studied the monkey's staff movements over a long period of time and finally applied these strange techniques to the five monkey forms he had developed.

The monkey staff techniques are completely different from the conventional stick-fighting techniques found in other kung-fu styles. Rather than the hard, rigid blows, the movements of the monkey staff are smooth and flowing, featuring strikes with speed and accuracy. The spinning and swinging motions of the staff, along with monkey screams and mimicry, confuse the opponent and leave him with no time to guess where the next blow will land.

The monkey staff is the most difficult weapon to learn. Mastery requires several years of hard work. It also demands the highest degree of flexibilty. The student must perfect the basic skills — swinging, striking, thrusting, and twirling — before he even attempts the staff form.

The student should use a strong, heavy staff when first learning the basic skills. It helps develop more strength in the swinging and hitting and builds up more speed and power. Later, a lightweight staff is recommended.

"Light art" is used extensively in the form. The practitioner must be able to jump extremely high, turn 360 degrees in the air and strike three blows to the opponent's body. He must also be able to jump up and out of the way of a sweep or low kick, and then come down blocking and striking with the staff.

The practitioner's internal power adds to the strength, balance, and power of the staff. He extends his chi up through his body, down the staff and out its end until the staff is not just an object but an extension of the body.

In performing the staff form, the master uses a silver staff to honor the great Sage Sun Wu Kung (Monkey King) of Chinese folklore.

Monkey staff

Keep your staff low to the ground as your opponent prepares to attack.

As he attacks, move in with the staff.

Knock his knife away with an upward block.

Turn the staff and strike across his head. Reach out to grab his weapon.

5

Throw his weapon to the ground.

6

He finally falls to the ground.

Monkey staff

1

Start farther from your opponent, with the staff at a higher angle.

2

As he attacks, block his sword strike with your staff.

Continue swinging the staff until you strike the sword and his head in one motion.

Swing the staff until you have knocked the sword from his hand. Pull back on the monkey staff and turn it around.

5

Strike across with the back side of the staff until you have delivered a fatal blow to his neck.

The Sword

When a practitioner advances into the realm of weaponry, the first weapon he learns is the sword. This same rule applies to monkey kung-fu. According to legend, Sun Wun Kung's first weapon was a sword, not a staff. By combining monkey movements with his knowledge of weaponry, Kou Sze originated the monkey sword form.

The monkey sword consists of a number of swinging patterns combined with ground rolling and acrobatic jumps. Like the monkey forms, the sword form is fast and furious. A great deal of time must be spent just learning the twirling of the sword.

Monkey sword

Start from a low monkey horse with the sword in front of you.

2

As he steps forward to strike, block up with the sword.

3

Sliding your blade across, grab his left wrist.

Keep his right arm down and pull his sword away.

Grab his knife and strike the neck area.

6

Stab him in the back.

The Monkey Rope

Another unusual weapon taken from the monkey's habitat is the monkey rope. Kou Sze watched the monkeys swinging from vine to vine. Many times they would pull the vines off the tree and use it to whip each other. Sometimes the vine would wrap around one of the monkey's legs and be tugged, causing the monkey to lose his balance.

The monkey rope form uses a long rope, similar to a vine, with a small weight attached to the end. When thrown properly, the rope wraps around the opponent's limb. The practitioner can pull him off balance, thus making him completely open to attack. By spinning and throwing the weighted end of the rope, it can strike an opponent from a distance. The rope can also be used to choke an opponent or tie him up.

Monkey rope

Start from a low position, holding the weighted monkey rope in your hands.

2

Swing the rope as your opponent begins his attack.

3

As your opponent throws a kick with his left leg, throw the rope and wrap it around his back leg.

4

Lean back and pull on the monkey rope.

5

Pull your opponent off balance by moving slightly higher.

He falls to the ground.

Jump into the air and aim for your opponent.

Come down on your opponent and strike to his head.

The Judge's Pen

The pointed cudgel or the judge's pen, another monkey style weapon, is a set of spinning daggers with a point on each end. Each dagger is attached to the practitioner by a ring placed on a finger. This prevents the dagger from falling when hit. The practitioner uses the judge's pen much as a monkey uses a stick to poke at his opponent.

Judge's pen

1

Begin in a low position, keeping the judge's pin in a blocking mode.

2

Block with your right hand as your opponent strikes with a front punch.

3

Step forward and jab him in the side with the left pin.

Second judge's pen

As your attacker throws a front kick, lean away from him.

Stab down at his left leg.

As he desperately tries to throw a punch, stab at his side.

Stepping high, bring up your right arm for a strike.

5

Apply a fatal strike to your attacker's side.

ABOUT THE AUTHORS

Paulie Zink

A master of tai shing pek kwar, Zink is an example of a person whose art is well-suited to his mind and body. The best monkey stylists have the ability to become convincingly monkeylike, and Zink possesses the agility and the elusive, elastic body the art requires.

Zink has been practicing tai shing pek kwar for over ten years and for at least six hours every day. He is completely devoted to his art, both physically and spiritually.

A three-time weapons grand champion at the annual Long Beach Internationals in California, Zink is known as the Western world's "Monkey King," and is considered among the foremost authorities on monkey kung-fu. He is also one of the most flexible practitioners in the martial arts.

Zink lives in Southern California, and teaches a small select group of students in the city of Glendale. He has also conducted a few seminars throughout the country and has appeared in several well-known martial art magazines. In 1982, he received the "Competitor of the Year" award from *Inside Kung-Fu* magazine.

Michael J. Gonzalez

A native of Southern California, Michael J. Gonzalez graduated from college with a degree in journalism. He has been practicing kung-fu for ten years and studies tai shing pek kwar under Paulie Zink. He is currently a freelance writer and photographer for several well-known martial art magazines.

UNIQUE LITERARY BOOKS OF THE WORLD